WINDOW ON A CATHOLIC PARISH

St Mary's, Granard, Co. Longford, 1933–68

Maynooth Studies in Local History

GENERAL EDITOR Raymond Gillespie

This pamphlet is one of five new additions to the Maynooth Studies in Local History series in 1996 and adds to an ever growing literature of local history in Ireland. The studies are all drawn from theses submitted as part of the Maynooth M.A. course in local history which began in 1992. Each essay is an exploration not of particular places, usually identified by administrative boundaries, but rather of how in the 'little places' of Ireland their inhabitants lived out their day-to-day lives in the past. As a result the range of subjects covered in these essays is as broad as the experience of any one or even a group of individuals.

Many things bound people together, and drove them apart, in the past and pressures for change came from both within and without regional societies. These bonds and divisions are reflected in these studies: religion at parish level, the comonalities of living in the same town, parish or landed estate, or places where they met each other, such as schools, or fought with each other, as at fairs. It is these complex realities which give the Irish historical experience its richness and diversity and which can only be fully appreciated at the local level and from a series of chronological and geographical perspectives.

These Maynooth Studies in Local History, like the earlier volumes in the series, help us to build more complex pictures of the reality of the Irish past from the middle ages to the present and in doing so presents local history as the vibrant and challenging discipline that it is.

IN THIS SERIES

Maynooth Studies in Local History: Number 8

Window on a Catholic Parish

St Mary's, Granard, Co. Longford, 1933-68

Francis Kelly

IRISH ACADEMIC PRESS

Set in 10 on 12 point Bembo by
Verbatim Typesetting & Design, Dublin
and published by
IRISH ACADEMIC PRESS LTD
Kill Lane, Blackrock, Co. Dublin, Ireland
and in North America by
IRISH ACADEMIC PRESS LTD
c/o ISBS, 5804 NE Hassalo Street, Portland, OR 97213

A catalogue record for this title
is available from the British Library.

ISBN 0-7165-2594-1

Printed in Ireland
by Colour Books, Dublin

Contents

Preface

It gives me great pleasure to record my indebtedness to and express my thanks to all who co-operated with me and helped me while I was researching and writing this essay:

To Professor R.V. Comerford, head of the Department of Modern History: as my supervisor, he has given me much-valued advice, assistance and encouragement.

To the course director, Dr Raymond Gillespie: he has provided a varied, stimulating and challenging programme over two academic years and assembled a talented, friendly and sympathetic staff to deliver it. To each of these, too, I offer my sincere thanks. They leave only happy memories.

To the officials of the National Archives, Bishop Street, Dublin, the Librarian and staff of the Library of St Patrick's College, Maynooth and the Librarian and Staff of Longford County Library: they have been cheerful, helpful and very efficient always.

To all those who gave interviews or helped to verify details of information or who put me in touch with oral or written sources.

To local historian, Dan Kennedy: he provided me with many useful hints – especially about sources – and helped to clarify many issues in late-night conversations.

To my bishop, Most Reverend Colm O'Reilly: he has taken a keen interest in the project and given me the benefit of his own inside-track information about the period I have researched.

To Geraldine Kelly and Anne Kelly for their word-processing skills and their patience.

To all the members of the MA in Local History class of 1993-5: I made so many new friends.

Introduction

Granard, the second town in county Longford, is situated in the north-eastern corner of the county on the road linking the midlands with Cavan and thence, through Monaghan and Armagh, with the principal towns and cities of Northern Ireland. The parish, to which Granard gives its name, covers an area of 14,529 acres[1] and has a population (at time of writing) of just under two thousand people.[2] In ecclesiastical terms, it is one of the four deanery towns of the diocese of Ardagh and Clonmacnois. The nineteenth century saw attempts being made by a succession of ener-getic and pastorally-minded bishops of the diocese of Ardagh and Clonmacnois to re-establish parish organisation and appropriate ecclesias-tical discipline.[3] Granard seems to have been one of the parishes where this campaign met with some degree of success. This is indicated, *inter alia*, by the fact that the parish has some of the oldest and best-kept parish reg-isters in the diocese.[4] The second half of the nineteenth century saw quite extraordinary achievements in the parish. Among the material successes there was the building of an elaborate new church (1860-7), a new parochial house (1869-70), five new primary schools (1885-92) and among the pastoral initiatives there was the introduction of parish missions (from 1867 onwards) confraternities, sodalities, a catechetical programme, devo-tional literature and any other available means of revitalising Catholic life. This momentum continued into the twentieth century. The records in the parish archive show that further property was procured, existing buildings were extended and improved and pastoral activity was intensi-fied.[5] One particular development, which has had far-reaching conse-quences, was the arrival in 1881 of the Sisters of Mercy. The Granard community was founded from Newtownforbes and came, initially, to help with nursing and teaching in Granard Union Workhouse, which had been opened in 1842. Since 1891 they have had charge of the girls' prima-ry school; they established a girls' secondary school in 1947, which became co-educational in 1959. They have also been involved in a wide variety of pastoral work, especially home visitation, coping with poverty and catechetical instruction.[6]

The subject of this essay is the thirty-five year pastorate of the Revd Denis O'Kane (1933-68). It is the longest pastorate in this century:

indeed, as far as can be established, it is the longest pastorate in the entire history of the parish. The period is a formative one in the history of the country. Every local community had to respond to the challenge of political turbulence, Economic War, World War, emigration, post-war social and economic change and, of course, change in religious thought and practice. Granard's parochial records are very complete for this period. It is possible to examine the administration of the parish and the maintenance of its properties, to establish what were the pastoral priorities and what initiatives were undertaken to achieve these, to identify and to estimate what were the factors that favoured the success or contributed to the failure of the various undertakings. But before discussing these sources some account will be given of the parish priest who created them and the curates who co-operated with and assisted him as well as of local conditions in the area in which they worked.

THE PASTORAL TEAM 1933-68

Denis, son of Denis O'Kane of Drumeel, Moatfarrell, county Longford and Mary Anne O'Hara, of Muckerstaff, Granard, county Longford was born on 2 July 1884.[7] He probably received his primary education at the one-roomed school in his native townland or in the townland of Castlebrock – both of which were closed and replaced by Clonbroney National School in the early 1920s. His secondary education was completed at St Mel's College, Longford, the diocesan minor seminary founded in 1865 by Bishop John Kilduff.[8] He entered St Patrick's College, Maynooth in 1902,[9] where he was ordained to the priesthood by Archbishop Walsh on 20th June 1909. After a year's post-graduate study he gained his licentiate in Theology (S.T.L.) in 1910[10] and returned to work in his native diocese of Ardagh and Clonmacnois. His first appointment was to Ardagh as assistant to the formidable Monsignor James O'Farrell.[11] In 1914 he was appointed to the teaching staff of St Mel's College, Longford and became its president in 1921.[12] On 1 January, 1933 he became parish priest of St Mary's, Granard, where he ministered until his death on the night of 3/4 March 1968.[13] He had been appointed a canon of the cathedral chapter by Bishop Joseph Hoare in 1922 and became, successively, archdeacon (1957), dean (1960) and vicar general (1962).[14]

Shortly after his arrival in Granard one of his assistants, Fr John Donlon, was transferred to Drumshambo, county Leitrim and was replaced on 1 February 1933 by Fr Thomas D. Sheeran.[15] The other assistant, Fr Peter O'Farrell, was soon appointed parish priest of Killashee, county Longford and was replaced on 31 March 1933 by Fr Patrick MacCormaic.[16] This partnership (of the three tall men) lasted until 1946 and during those years the pattern was established of pastoral practice, parish administration and clerical involvement in local affairs which was to last until the late 1960s.

Fr Sheeran was transferred to Drumshambo, county Leitrim on 16 January 1946 and was replaced by Fr Edward O'Carroll.[17] His very popular and successful ministry came to a sudden and untimely end when he died in the District Hospital, Mohill, county Leitrim on 22 October, 1952 from injuries sustained in a road accident which occurred while he was returning from a friend's funeral in Cloone, county Leitrim.[18] This tragedy touched Canon O'Kane very deeply; he felt the loss of his esteemed colleague and trusted friend profoundly and penned a very feeling tribute to him in his annual report for that year.[19] Fr MacCormaic remained in Granard until his transfer to Mohill, county Leitrim, on 23 June 1948 when he was replaced by Fr Donal O'Lehane.[20] Fr O'Carroll was replaced briefly (30 October 1952 to 7 February 1953) by Fr Michael Egan, who had just recently returned from Australia where he had worked in various capacities and positions since his ordination to the priesthood in 1936.[21] He was more permanently replaced by Fr Patrick James Woods who ministered in Granard from 7 February 1953 to 14 January 1964.[22] On 14 July 1960 Fr O'Lehane was transferred to Loughduff, county Cavan (parish of Mullahoran) and was replaced by a newly ordained priest, Fr Colm O'Reilly (now bishop of Ardagh and Clonmacnois).[23] On the appointment of Fr Woods to the parish of Bornacoola, county Leitrim on 14 January 1964, his place was taken by Fr Francis O'Hanlon.[24] These last two named were Canon O'Kane's assistants at the time of his death. Fr O'Reilly, in particular, had become the friend and trusted companion of his old age, and was, after his death, the executor of his will.[25] All these were men of considerable and very varied talents and interests. It is a measure of Canon O'Kane's ability that he recognised, organised, directed, guided, even disciplined these talents without giving rise to a hint of discord or friction.

By nature and temperament he was a meticulously careful and prudent administrator. He had learned, during his eleven years as president of St Mel's College, where resources were always meagre enough, the importance of careful planning, accurate accounting and personal vigilance. The key to understanding his character and outlook on life is that his background was in farming. His family, though by no means wealthy, was comfortable and had considerably improved its lot during the life-time of his father. He admired those who worked hard and with perseverance, believing this way of life to be healthy and wholesome physically, mentally and spiritually. He detested waste or ostentation on the one hand and laziness or improvidence on the other. He regularly drew attention to what he considered the inefficient running of the town (or the country), the culture of dependence encouraged by 'hand outs' and the dishonest methods used to procure them.[26] He was not one to remain silent whenever he considered that an issue of principle was at stake: indeed his detractors regularly accused him of making every issue an issue of principle.[27]

THE VINEYARD – GRANARD IN 1933 AND AFTER

The town of Granard was in a state of decay in 1933 – 'a forlorn spectacle' is how its new parish priest described it.[28] His observations are supported by, among other sources, the archive of Granard Urban District Council.[29] The Council was having great difficulty in discharging its statutory obligations through lack of financial resources. Its area of jurisdiction was too small to yield the necessary revenue and its unpopularity was growing as it attempted to strike a realistic rate each year. As early as 14 June 1922 the town clerk had written to the Department of Local Government enclosing a petition from the ratepayers for deurbanisation.[30] The absence of a suitable legal framework (which, it seems, came only with the Local Government Act of 1925) meant the answer was in the negative.[31] Matters went from one crisis to another through the 1920s, 1930s and 1940s until an order was made by the Minister for Local Government and Public Health on 9 January 1942 dissolving of Granard Urban District Council and appointing Patrick Francis Patten, of 'Rathlin', Dublin Road, Malahide, to perform the duties of the District Council at a remuneration of £25 per annum, payable out of local funds and, in addition, travelling and subsistence expenses.[32] The de-urbanisation order was signed by the Minister for Local Government and Public Health on 6 January 1944 under Section 74 of the Local Government Act 1925 and came into operation on 1 April 1944. From that date the Granard Urban District Council was replaced by the Granard Town Commissioners. Thereafter Longford County Council became responsible for almost all the services hitherto provided by Granard Urban District Council and the costs of these became a charge on the county-at-large.

Canon O'Kane described in detail the living conditions of many of his flock: 'first and worst I put the old workhouse premises, a den of filth, moral and material … There is no general water supply and no system of sewerage in the town. The famous Ball-Alley is a hideous eyesore.'[33] This may appear harsh language but it is, in fact, moderate when compared with that used in the reports prepared by the Medical Inspector, Dr MacDonnell.[34] The atmosphere in the town was one of pessimism and the reports from the farming areas of the parish were no more promising. 'The fairs … are only a shadow of former greatness – small, bad prices, poor demand, great uncertainty as to the future.'[35] Clearly, therefore, his appointment was a challenging one but, with the support of his two assistants, he set to work on a variety of fronts. He was forty-eight years of age and in good health; his assistants were aged forty-three and thirty-three respectively, both vigorous, outdoor types. By the standards of the time it was a young team and, if, perhaps, conservative in temperament, it was, nevertheless, dedicated, enthusiastic and ably led. While the main focus of its activities was certainly spiritual and pastoral in the strict sense, each of the priests, and especially the assistants, engaged at different times in a wide variety of parochial activities ranging from music and drama through football and athletics to hunting and even hare-coursing. This pattern of involvement, established in the early years, continued and expanded right through the period.

THE SOURCES FOR THIS STUDY

The Catholic Church has always been concerned with the keeping of appropriate records, not only of baptisms, confirmations, marriages and deaths, but also of events of importance in the life of the parish or diocesan communities. Canon Law, as well as diocesan and provincial statutes of different dates, enjoins on bishops and parish priests the obligation of recording, and preserving in suitable archives, contemporary accounts of their day-to-day activities. The way in which this obligation is usually fulfilled is by keeping what are called the 'Chronicon' and the 'Parish Inventory Book'. For reasons of history (and for other reasons related to human frailty, lack of self-confidence or even laziness) this canonical legislation has not always been complied with in Ireland.

Canon O'Kane's pastorate is a notable exception. His great respect for the law, his keen mind and ready pen, as well as his attention to detail, ensured the creation of exceptional records. For each of the thirty-five years of his pastorate, he wrote a lengthy annual report detailing all the events of parish life – great and small, pleasant and unpleasant. These reports, running to 161 pages of closely written manuscript, give a very comprehensive picture of the social and economic, as well as the cultural and religious life of the parish. They indicate the efforts of priests and people together to cope with the challenges of life at a time when modern Ireland was in an adolescent phase of its development, still unsure of its future, and only gradually growing in confidence and towards maturity. They are frequently enlivened by the incisive (even sardonic) comments of their author and they contain unexpected, but precious, pieces of general information preserved in their *obiter dicta*, for example, the weekly rent (3s. 3d.) paid to Granard Urban District Council for each of the thirty-two new houses opened that year on the Scrabby Road (and later named St Colmcille's Terrace).[36] The officials of Longford County Council (the successor of Granard Urban District Council) do not have this information. The tone is dispassionate and objective – almost clinical – as befitted one who was a mathematician and logician. Perhaps, the most extraordinary single record they contain is that of a survey made in 1939 of the patterns of religious practice in the parish. This will receive special attention in the third chapter. The parish inventory book, which he found well-kept and up-to-date, he maintained and used to compile his report for the triennial episcopal visitations.

The account books of the parish and the records of clerical income document the material side of the long pastorate, while the records of baptisms, confirmations, marriages and deaths, the church notice books and sick-call books, as well as the schedule of church services, provide a detailed picture of the priests' spiritual ministrations.

A useful guide to the workings of local government over the period is provided by a collection of documents known collectively as the de-urbanisation file. These show the continuing efforts of the Granard Urban District Council to meet its statutory obligations. They show, too, the growing realisation that only through the abolition of this body and the vesting of its responsibilities in Longford County Council was there any hope of maintaining essential services and providing for much needed improvements.

The approach taken here is thematic rather than chronological. In the first chapter the material side of parish life is examined. Population trends and family size are described. Financial affairs – income and expenditure – are looked at and the personal revenue of the clergy themselves and its sources are analysed. The second chapter looks at the clergy's spiritual ministration of the parishioners from birth to death using as a guide the statistics provided by parish registers and other records like the sick-calls book. The third chapter, based on the data from the 1939 survey, describes the patterns of religious practice and seeks to relate these to the prevailing structures and emphases. Tables 1 to 11 are derived from the appropriate volumes of the parish registers of baptisms, confirmations, marriages and deaths. They are acknowledged here but not otherwise annotated in the text.

As noted by the editors of the *Directory of Irish Archives*[37] there is very little material available in the diocesan archive held at St Mel's, Longford after 1895. The reason for this is a decision made by the three executors of the will of Bishop MacNamee[38] to destroy all the records generated during his long episcopate (1927 to 1966) so that his successor, (who was expected to be from outside the diocese), would assume office without the advantage of too much knowledge. This accounts for the fact that no use could be made of the diocesan archive in this study.

Material Things: Parish Administration

According to canon law 'a parish is a certain community of Christ's faithful, stably established within a particular Church, whose pastoral care, under the authority of the diocesan Bishop, is entrusted to a parish priest as its proper pastor'.[1] The first element in a parish, therefore, is its people. The number of those in any particular parish may vary considerably from less than 500, which would be a small population even for one pastor, to several thousands, which would require a number of curates in addition to a parish priest. The norm of the diocese of Ardagh and Clonmacnois was a ratio of one priest to 1,000 members of congregation. Granard parish, which during the period covered by this study always had three priests for a congregation of 2,500 and dropping, fared better than the average. There was no shortage of work. They had two churches, a convent chapel, five primary schools, a secondary school and a vocational school to look after and the personal pastoral needs of individual parishioners to serve. The second element – that the community be stably established – implies provision, ownership (or trusteeship) and maintenance of property thus involving priests and people together in the guardianship of material things. Since the diocesan clergy of the Catholic Church in Ireland are non-stipendary and have, in general, no personal partimony, they derive their living entirely from the voluntary offerings of their people. To elicit these in sufficient quantity to provide a modest income further involves a parish priest with material things since he must motivate his congregation to provide for his own needs and those of his curate(s) where these are present.

PARISH POPULATION TRENDS

Since the beginning of this century it has been the practice in the diocese of Ardagh and Clonmacnois to assemble population statistics for each parish every five years. The method of collection is not uniform and there may sometimes be a margin of error. This makes comparisons of one parish with another difficult and unsatisfactory. It would seem, however, that, even before the period under review, Granard parish statistics were accurately recorded and preserved. Thus, the new parish priest in his first annual report (1933), is able to state that 'the Catholic population at the

last Census is given as 2,586'.² On seven occasions during Canon O'
Kane's pastorate this figure was corrected and updated. The parish archive
contains the field books used on these occasions. For the purpose of enu-
meration the parish was divided into 'town' and 'country' areas and the
names of those in each household recorded. From this the total population
was computed. Note was taken of the number of non-Catholics, though
names and number of households were not recorded.

Table 1 gives the results for the years of this survey. The total population shows a slow but steady decline over the entire period. The most significant decline occurred between 1940 and 1945 (115) and between 1955
and 1960 (162). It is tempting to speculate why this should be. The annual
report for 1941 gives an indication of what the contemporary understanding was. 'And meantime large numbers of young, and not so young, men
– fifteen in one morning – were going to England, attracted by the seem-
ingly wonderful wages offered by touts who made a good thing out of this
new export. A number soon came back disillusioned'.³ In relation to the
later period it might be suggested that the more widespread availability of
second level education made it inevitable that young people would emigrate in search of more suitable employment. Vocational education, after a
few false starts, had been established from 1950 and the Sisters of Mercy
had a small secondary school for girls from 1947 until 1959 when it was
expanded to become a co-educational secondary school. The annual report
for 1955 tells us that 'very many of our young people, especially girls, are
emigrating – chiefly to England'.⁴ Overall, there was a population decline
of 19.5 per cent. However, this was not uniform over the whole parish.
The rural areas lost much more heavily than the town area. The figures
were 28.9 per cent for the former as against 7.8 per cent for the latter. This
is explained, at least in part, by the depressed state of agriculture during the
period. The Economic War had brought financial ruin to many small
farmers, who made up the bulk of the rural population of the parish, and
the employment of farm labourers became a luxury they could no longer
afford. The drop in the non-Catholic population was even more dramatic
at 34.5 per cent. The changed political climate as well as the unfavourable
economic environment may have contributed to this. Table 5 below
shows that the excess of births over deaths for the period was 623. When
this factor is taken into account it makes the overall population drop of 490
seem even more alarming.

The decrease in overall population is paralleled by a decline in the
number of households. Overall, the number fell by 8.2 per cent: the
country areas suffered the heaviest loss of 13.2 per cent while in the town
the number of households was down by only 2.5 per cent. Family size
hardly changed at all over the years of our survey. The town average 4.6
dropped by 0.2 per cent while the country average of 3.8 did not alter at

all. While we have an average family size of 4.6 in the town, there are wide varations. A field-book of census-figures collected over this century records, for example, Michael Smith, born in September 1870, and married to Kate Brady, born in February 1876, as having a family of fifteen children born between 1891 and 1922. The second youngest of these, Joseph Smith, born in 1917, married Mary Reilly, born in 1923, and had a family of fourteen born between 1940 and 1958.[5]

		Table 1 Parish Population		
Year	*Town*	*Country*	*Total*	*Non-Catholic*
1935	1127	1390	2517	55
1940	1125	1387	2512	60
1945	1092	1305	2397	55
1950	1056	1274	2330	51
1955	1057	1195	2252	45
1960	967	1123	2090	43
1965	1039	988	2027	36

Families 1935	Town: 245	Country: 365	Total: 610
Families 1955	Town: 239	Country: 317	Total: 556

1935 Average Family Size:	Town: 4.6	Country: 3.8	Parish: 4.2
1955 Average Family Size:	Town: 4.4	Country: 3.8	Parish: 4.1

INCOME AND EXPENDITURE

The day-to-day financing of the parish can be examined by reference to Table 2. This shows the annual income and expenditure and the annual balances (credit or debit) over the period. These can be converted to current (1995) values by reference to Nett Present Value (N.P.V.). This is the most useful common valuation known: 'The present value of a future sum of money is simply that sum of money that, if you were to receive it today, would, when invested at the average rate of interest, accumulate to the pre-stated future value.'[6] In the real world inflation also exists, so account must be taken of this. By the use of statistics extrapolated by the Central Bank of Ireland, Table 2 was calculated showing the constant 1995 values of income/expenditure for the years 1933-67. In its crudest form the calculation used to derive present day value of previous years' incomes/expenditures is as follows: Value of 1933 income/expenditure today equals

Value at 1927 prices $\times \dfrac{1933 \text{ Value at } 1995 \text{ prices}}{1933 \text{ Value at } 1927 \text{ prices}}$

using: 1) 1927 as the base year and
           2) The first five months of 1995 as our 1995 price.

Example   1933 Income in 1995 value $620 \times \dfrac{6283.20}{151} = £25,798.57$

          1933 Expenditure in 1995 value $272 \times \dfrac{6283.20}{151} = £11,318.08$

In all but one year (1934) a small working surplus is recorded. This, however, is not the complete picture. No clear-cut distinction was drawn
between 'current' and 'capital' expenditure and, given the usually small
size of the excess of current income over current expenditure, no prudent
planning could be made for capital outlay (especially major repairs), the
need for which might easily have been foreseen. Accordingly, when any
such capital outlay became absolutely necessary there was a financial crisis
which had to be met by special appeals and exceptional collections. This
explains the somewhat erratic nature of annual income and expenditure.
For example, the sudden increase in income in 1940 and 1941 (matched
by an equally steep rise in expenditure) is explained by the fact that the
roof of the church, extensively damaged by a windstorm, had to be com-
pletely replaced. The annual report for 1940 details the shock experienced
alike by parish priest and people at the discovery by the architect, Mr H.
Bryne, that the entire roof needed to be renewed. 'The architect pointed
out these defects at each visit he made and pleaded with me to undertake
an over-haul of the entire roof. Naturally, I shrank from such a formidable
undertaking in the middle of a World War when materials were so hard
to procure and the price of them, and of labour, was so much advanced'.[7]
The cost of repairing storm-damage had been estimated, initially, at £413.
Now the parish was faced with an outlay of at least £3,000 to renew the
entire roof of the church. An urgent appeal for direct contributions
brought in £1,580 before the end of 1940. The work was finished in
October 1941 at a total cost of £3,425.63. In 1949 it was the turn of the
heating system; in 1951 new seating was provided and by 1955 the damp
walls (which architect, parish priest, contractor and all concerned felt sure
would have been cured by the new roof and other repairs) had to be
addressed. With this explanation one can see from Table 2 not only the
current income and expenditure levels but also the periods when capital
expenditure made the greatest demands on parish resources.

Table 2 Income and Expenditure

Year	Income		Expenditure		Balance	
	£	£ 1995 values	£	£ 1995 values	£	£ 1995 values
1933	620	25,799	272	11,318	348	14,481
1934	674	27,861	730	30,179	-56	-2,318
1935	777	31,295	616	24,811	161	6,484
1936	533	20,931	404	15,865	129	5,066
1937	547	20,217	357	13,195	190	7,022
1938	1,183	42,965	796	28,910	387	14,055
1939	739	26,086	358	12,637	381	13,049
1940	2,363	72,425	1,198	36,718	1,165	35,707
1941	2,602	72,340	2,451	68,187	151	4,153
1942	1,897	47,672	902	22,670	995	25,002
1943	1,883	42,104	941	21,041	942	21,063
1944	1,407	29,983	666	14,186	741	15,797
1945	1,235	26,392	413	8,826	822	17,566
1946	1,114	24,140	456	9,882	658	14,258
1947	1,457	29,820	588	12,034	869	17,786
1948	1,486	29,453	608	29,453	878	17,402
1949	2,297	45,389	1,617	31,952	680	13,437
1950	1,574	30,709	497	9,696	1,077	21,013
1951	2,028	6,626	1,540	29,812	488	6,814
1952	1,773	29,471	1,239	20,592	534	8,879
1953	1,284	20,270	652	10,295	632	9,975
1954	1,741	27,402	713	11,222	1,028	16,180
1955	1,903	29,192	1,276	19,574	627	9,618
1956	2,769	40,745	2,623	38,597	146	2,148
1957	1,080	15,263	744	10,514	336	4,749
1958	1,561	21,124	1,472	19,919	89	1,205
1959	1,409	19,036	1,209	16,358	200	2,678
1960	1,648	22,201	1,313	17,688	335	4,513
1961	2,143	28,095	1,947	25,525	196	2,570
1962	2,635	33,132	1,387	17,440	1,248	15,692
1963	3,447	42,301	2,415	29,636	1,032	12,665
1964	4,314	49,607	4,049	46,559	265	3,048
1965	2,472	27,063	2,205	27,939	267	2,922
1966	2,806	29,832	2,552	27,131	254	2,701
1967	2,042	21,050	1,049	10,814	975	10,236

INCOME OF THE CLERGY AND ITS SOURCES

During all of his pastorate, Canon O'Kane had two curates. The three
shared a parochial house built in 1868 and located in the centre of the
town (convenient for the people, but with the disadvantage of being some
distance from the church). They depended for their living on the dona-
tions of the parishioners taken at various times throughout the year and on
various pretexts. Table 3 shows the gross income for each year and Table
4 shows the various sources of income and their relative importance using
two particular years, 1935 and 1955 as typical. The figures in Table 3 have
been converted to 1995 values using the N.P.V. Revenue was divided
between the parish priest and his two curates in the ratio 3:1:1. The explanation for this apparent injustice was that the parish priest had responsibility for a number of domestic outlays. For example, he paid the
housekeepers.[8] (In a parochial house with three priests there were usually
two housekeepers – one experienced, the other apprenticed). He also
provided light and heat. He was responsible, personally, for certain enter-
tainment like that of the bishop at confirmation time, the schools' inspec-
tors or government officials on business, or the professionals called in for
various services. The curates made a contribution in lieu of their board
and lodgings, laundry etc. varying from £1 to £2 per week over the
period.[9] By examining the figures in Table 3 (expressed in 1995 values) it
also emerges that the gross income of the parish clergy over the period of
this survey was at least as high, and most times higher, than it is today.

The obvious fluctuations – sometimes quite considerable – in the
annual gross total are explained by the erratic nature of one of the most
important sources of income, namely funeral offerings.[10] This meant that
at each funeral of an adult in the parish, a collection was taken up for the
support of the clergy before the remains left the church for burial. The
family of the deceased made the largest contribution and each of those
present made a lesser contribution depending on the closeness of his/her
relationship or other association with the deceased. This method of col-
lecting revenue seems to have belonged entirely to the Armagh province.
Elsewhere in Ireland stole-fees seem to have accounted for a much more
significant part of the priest' revenue. The practice ceased in the diocese
of Ardagh and Clonmacnoise on St Patrick's Day, 1972. Table 4 shows
the proportion of total revenue from this source to be 45 per cent in 1935
and 37 per cent in 1955. The next in order of importance after Funeral
Offerings were the collections, variously known as 'offerings' or 'dues',
taken at Christmas, Easter and November and accounting for 33.5 per
cent of the total in 1935 and 36.2 per cent in 1955. The other collections
together accounted for a quarter or less of the gross annual income.

The picture that emerges is of a community that had to struggle hard

Table 3 Annual Clergy Income

Year	Income £	£ 1995 values
1933	653	27,172
1934	728	30,093
1935	782	30,208
1936	840	32,987
1937	826	30,529
1938	756	27,457
1939	640	22,591
1940	807	24,734
1941	672	18,683
1942	910	22,871
1943	837	18,715
1944	1,121	23,876
1945	1,059	22,632
1946	982	21,276
1947	1,035	21,183
1948	1,217	24,122
1949	1,269	25,074
1950	1,384	27,006
1951	1,727	31,181
1952	1,299	21,592
1953	1,598	25,228
1954	1,356	20,801
1955	1,950	30,692
1956	1,612	23,720
1957	1,818	25,692
1958	1,702	23,033
1959	1,903	25,747
1960	2,241	30,190
1961	1,664	21,814
1962	2,233	28,078
1963	1,796	22,040
1964	2,360	27,138
1965	1,995	21,842
1966	2,014	21,412
1967	2,370	24,432

Table 4 Sources of Income £

		Year	
		1935	1955
1	Offerings collected at Christmas, Easter and November	262.00	707.00
2	Offerings collected at Station Masses in Spring and Autumn	60.00	163.00
3	Offerings collected at Funerals	354.00	725.00
4	Offerings collected as 'Oats Money' (in spring)	42.00	171.00
5	Stole Fees (Baptisms and Wedings)	34.00	124.00
6	Donation from Sisters of Mercy for Chaplaincy services	30.00	60.00
	Total	782.00	1,950.00

to maintain itself and of a leadership that was very conscious of the extent of this struggle. The failure of native government to bring about the expected social and economic improvements led to dissillusionment and many took what appeared to be the easier and better option – they emigrated in search of a prosperity that often eluded them. Canon O'Kane frequently lamented this. Conscious of the difficulties facing his parishioners, he refrained from putting any avoidable burden on them and by careful administration of finances and avoiding all but absolutely essential spending, he managed to maintain a modest credit balalnce during all the years of his pastorate. Similarly, by living frugally (which was very much in his nature anyway) he avoided making demands for personal income on his parishioners which he would have seen as excessive. It could be argued that he was too cautious; that, in fact, the resources were never quite so meagre as he assumed and that a more imaginative and inventive approach to fundraising could have generated greater income and allowed for a more ambitious capital programme during his lifetime, thus avoiding the need for major expenditure after his death.

Spiritual Things: Parish Ministry

Table 5 details certain very important elements of spiritual ministration in the parish. There was an average of forty-nine baptisms each year from a high of sixty-one in 1948 to a low of thirty-seven in each of the years 1940 and 1966. This meant that there was a regular supply of new members of the Catholic community and gave some hope for the future even if it might be prudently foreseen that many of these would leave to live elsewhere in Ireland or would emigrate in their late teens or early twenties. The need to prepare young people to survive as Catholics in a more challenging environment gave added importance to catechetical instruction. It also meant, among other things, that schools had a fairly steady supply of pupils and accounts for the fact that, though there was some variation within the catchment areas of the three country schools, there was comparatively little difficulty in maintaining the numbers required to keep the schools open and retain their staffs.[1] It also justified the regular, on-going expenditure on the primary schools which was a recurring feature of parish administration. The number of deaths, averaging thirty-one per year, was always less than the number of births, so, in theory, the population should have been rising. Emigration and migration prevented this from happening, in practice, so that, as already noted above, there was a substantial population drop over the entire period.

The bishop's triennial visitation was the occasion of the confirmation of an average of 151 children and from 1945 onward the parish priest was granted faculties to confirm in danger of death so a new statistic – those confirmed by the parish priest – appears in the confirmation register from that date. Confirmation day was one of the great events in the parish and was prepared for by clergy, teachers, parents and children with meticulous care. 'His lordship, the bishop, came for visitation on 17 and 18 May 1939. On the 17th he examined the children and expressed himself as very well pleased indeed – the best he had met this year. On the 18th he confirmed 146 (eighty-one boys, sixty-four girls and one adult – a recent convert). He spoke again of his pleasure at finding christian doctrine so very well taught: at observing that churches, schools and parochial buildings were so well kept. He exhorted to better attendance at Sunday Mass and Sodalities, and warned again about occasions of sin and scandal.'[2]

Table 5

Year	Baptisms	Marriages	Deaths	*Confirmations
1933	50	5	26	160
1934	60	11	27	
1935	54	13	33	
1936	42	11	37	135
1937	50	10	36	
1938	47	13	27	
1939	50	10	23	146
1940	37	12	31	
1941	43	13	29	
1942	51	11	32	142
1943	53	7	40	
1944	43	9	47	(3)
1945	60	11	30	123
1946	46	13	26	
1947	56	10	24	
1948	61	11	32	128 (3)
1949	49	6	32	
1950	47	11	32	(4)
1951	48	9	41	138 (2)
1952	47	8	31	
1953	57	8	34	
1954	54	6	36	188
1955	51	8	26	
1956	48	7	40	(2)
1957	47	5	27	119
1958	48	9	31	(1)
1959	48	0	30	(1)
1960	44	3	30	159
1961	39	3	26	
1962	46	5	34	
1963	50	4	30	170
1964	44	4	26	
1965	45	8	27	
1966	37	8	29	180 (1)
1967	56	8	23	
Totals	1,708	290	1,085	1,768

* For Confirmations, numbers in brackets denote those confirmed by the Parish Priest in emergency situations.

Marriages were never very numerous and, especially in the last quarter of our period, dwindled to the point where no marriage at all was celebrated in the year 1959. The reasons for this were mainly economic. It was harder to make a living, particularly on the small farms that were typical of the parish and no worthwhile industrial development had taken place locally. The brightest and best were leaving – especially the girls. It took considerable courage for those who remained to propose marriage. One substantial quotation, from the annual report of 1951, must serve to illustrate the atmosphere of depression (although for number of marriages this was one of the better years):

> Marriages numbered only 10 and of those only a few in the country districts. As against this, marriage papers were sent to 21 young people – 15 boys and 6 girls – for marriages elsewhere – 15 in England, 3 in USA, 1 in Northern Ireland, 1 in Dublin, 1 in Australia. The unfortunate small farmer, with less than fifteen acres, cannot get a girl to face the economic hardships of life on such a small holding and without any hope of help. Actually, such holdings are disappearing rapidly – for this and other reasons – and the wretched houses on such farms have fallen, the land being acquired by a well-to-do neighbour or purchased as an 'out-farm' by some merchant or farmer.[3]

The same annual report enumerates a total of sixty-one houses in the country areas of the parish which have disappeared since 1933.

BAPTISMS

Table 6 shows that the total number of children born into the families of the parish over our thirty-five year period was 1,708, or an average of 49 per year. Of these 934, or 54.7 per cent, were boys and 774, or 45.3 per cent were girls. At the beginning of the period almost all babies were born at home and christened (usually within the first three days after birth) in the parish church. Later, however, and especially towards the end of the period many of the babies were born in some of the Dublin maternity hospitals (the Coombe and Holles Street), in Longford hospital and in a variety of privately-owned nursing homes, particularly in Longford, Newtownforbes and Edgeworthstown. This reflects a better standard of health-care for expectant mothers and also, in some instances at least, better economic circumstances since, in the privately-owned nursing homes, and in the public hospitals, except for the very poor, care had to be paid for. In 1933, out of a total of fifty baptisms, only two were cele-

Table 6 Baptisms

Year	St Mary's		Elsewhere		Combined		Combined Total
	Boys	Girls	Boys	Girls	Boys	Girls	
1933	28	20	2	0	30	20	50
1934	31	24	4	1	35	25	60
1935	26	28	0	0	26	28	54
1936	20	17	3	2	23	19	42
1937	22	20	4	4	26	24	50
1938	23	20	1	3	24	23	47
1939	24	21	3	2	27	23	50
1940	17	17	2	1	19	18	37
1941	15	23	4	1	19	24	43
1942	26	20	2	3	28	23	51
1943	22	22	4	5	26	27	53
1944	23	16	1	3	24	19	43
1945	26	24	6	4	32	28	60
1946	23	18	3	2	26	20	46
1947	25	23	4	4	29	27	56
1948	23	25	11	2	34	27	61
1949	27	17	4	1	31	18	49
1950	25	14	6	2	31	16	47
1951	24	15	3	6	27	21	48
1952	21	17	6	3	27	20	47
1953	24	21	7	5	31	26	57
1954	22	23	2	7	24	30	54
1955	31	12	4	4	35	16	51
1956	17	21	8	2	25	23	48
1957	21	13	9	4	30	17	47
1958	16	17	11	4	27	21	48
1959	15	15	10	8	25	23	48
1960	20	10	9	5	29	15	44
1961	10	13	11	5	21	18	39
1962	17	13	12	4	29	17	46
1963	20	18	6	6	26	24	50
1964	17	11	11	5	28	16	44
1965	15	16	2	12	17	28	45
1966	9	18	6	4	15	22	37
1967	22	23	6	5	28	28	56
Total	747	645	187	129	934	774	1,708

Table 7 Marriages – Where did the Brides find their Husbands?

Year	In the Parish	Outside the Parish	Total
1933	2	3	5
1934	7	4	11
1935	10	3	13
1936	7	4	11
1937	5	5	10
1938	6	7	13
1939	5	5	10
1940	7	5	12
1941	5	8	13
1942	6	5	11
1943	2	5	7
1944	7	2	9
1945	8	3	11
1946	8	5	13
1947	6	4	10
1948	5	6	11
1949	5	1	6
1950	6	5	11
1951	5	4	9
1952	3	5	8
1953	2	6	8
1954	4	2	6
1955	0	8	8
1956	3	4	7
1957	3	2	5
1958	5	4	9
1959	0	0	0
1960	0	3	3
1961	1	2	3
1962	2	3	5
1963	0	4	4
1964	2	2	4
1965	3	5	8
1966	5	3	8
1967	4	4	8
Totals	149	141	290

brated outside the parish, while in 1964, out of a total of forty-four baptisms, sixteen were celebrated outside. Over the entire period 316, or 18.5
per cent of the total, were christened in other parishes. While it might be
argued that this reduced the work-load of the parish clergy, it also had
financial implications: stole-fees were given to the priests who celebrated
the baptisms, thus reducing the income available to support the Granard
clergy. 'Edgeworthstown and Newtownforbes now have Nursing Homes
– to add to the supply ... and very often baptism is conferred away from
home'.[4]

MARRIAGES

Table 7 indicates that a total of 290 marriages were solemnised in St
Mary's Church between 1933 and 1967. In just over half of these, 149 in
all, both parties came from the parish. The other 141 brides found their
husbands mostly in the surrounding parishes and the marriage in Granard
of a local girl to a man from a distant part of the country or from abroad
was exceptional. On the other hand, the annual reports make frequent
references to marriage papers being sent abroad to boys and girls who
sometimes were married soon to partners from the countries where they
lived and worked.[5] This strengthens the contention that the reason for late
marriage or no marriage at home was economic.

It is more difficult to be specific about where the young men who
married found their wives. On the basis that nearly half the young women
found husbands outside the parish – which suggests that the young men of
neighbouring parishes were coming in – it might reasonable be speculated
that at least a like proportion of young men would have found wives outside their immediate neighbourhood.

The fact of marriage in a Catholic Church is always to be notified to

Table 8 Marriages Age at Marriage (to nearest year)		
	Men	*Women*
Up to 20	6	48
21–30	112	157
31–40	109	60
41–50	53	22
51–60	8	3
Over 60	2	0
Total	290	290

the place of baptism of the party. It is entered in the baptismal register of that parish as a marginal note. The marriage register of the parish where the marriage takes place should contain a marginal note that this has been done. By examining these latter marginal notes it is possible to deduce the age of the party at the time of his/her marriage. Table 8 gives the results of this analysis for the period of our study. It suggests nothing unexpected. The bulk of those who married, sixty-seven per cent of men and seventy-five per cent of women, married between the ages of twenty-one and forty. Among the men 39 per cent married between the ages of 21 and 30 while 38 per cent married between thirty-one and forty. Among the women a much higher proportion, 54 per cent, married between the ages of twenty-one and thirty, while only 21 per cent of brides were aged thirty-one to forty. There were very few marriages of elderly people and, among the men, almost as few very young marriages. Forty-eight girls married under twenty years of age. There are two suggested reasons – firstly, local 'intelligence' alleges that match-making accounts for a fair proportion of them: in difficult economic circumstances a young girl might be 'persuaded' to accept an older man of substance with 'prospects'. Secondly, there is evidence that some of them were *'ex necessitate et post crimen'*.[6] This last forms a recurring theme in the annual report. The report of Fr Columbus O.F.M.Cap. to Canon O'Kane after the parish mission of 1938 would certainly reinforce this view.[7]

DEATHS

During the whole period of our survey, 1,085 deaths are recorded, giving an annual average for the period of thirty-one. The highest number of deaths, forty-seven in all, occurred in 1944: the lowest, only twenty-three, occurred in the years 1939 and 1967. Table 9 shows the numbers of men and women who died over these years – 571 or 52.6 per cent were men and 514 or 47.4 per cent were women. Turning to the ages at which people died (Table 10) we see that mortality in the younger age-groups was not very common. Only nineteen people died in their teens and even the numbers in the age-group twenty to thirty-nine years, seventy-six in all, is not very high when one considers the prevalence of tuberculosis, diphtheria and other killer diseases in the earlier years. By far, the biggest group, 567 or 52 per cent in all belonged to the age-group sixty to seventy-nine. The oldest recorded death for the period is that of Elizabeth Kiernan, The Hill, aged ninety-eight years and the youngest is that of John O'Hara, Main Street, aged thirteen months. It may be that deaths of infants, even those who died after baptism were not always recorded: more research in family history is needed to establish the accuracy of the

Table 9 Deaths

Year	Men	Women	Total
1933	11	15	26
1934	17	10	27
1935	17	16	33
1936	18	19	37
1937	17	19	36
1938	18	9	27
1939	14	9	23
1940	14	17	31
1941	14	15	29
1942	13	19	32
1943	19	21	40
1944	25	22	47
1945	18	12	30
1946	9	17	26
1947	10	14	24
1948	20	12	32
1949	19	13	32
1950	15	17	32
1951	17	24	41
1952	21	10	31
1953	16	18	34
1954	18	18	36
1955	14	12	26
1956	19	21	40
1957	14	13	27
1958	17	14	31
1959	20	10	30
1960	14	16	30
1961	17	9	26
1962	15	19	34
1963	20	10	30
1964	13	13	26
1965	15	12	27
1966	19	10	29
1967	14	9	23
Totals	571	514	1,085

	Up to 19	20-39	40-59	60-79	80-99	100 +	Total
			Table 10 Deaths – Age at Time of Death				
1933	I	4	7	8	6		26
1934	I	3	2	15	6		27
1935	I	I	6	20	5		33
1936	–	8	6	16	7		37
1937	I	4	4	19	8		36
1938	–	4	4	13	6		27
1939	I	–	4	15	3		23
1940	I	4	7	12	7		31
1941	–	2	2	18	7		29
1942	I	–	4	20	7		32
1943	–	6	9	14	11		40
1944	2	6	11	17	11		47
1945	–	4	2	17	7		30
1946	–	–	4	13	9		26
1947	2	2	3	12	5		24
1948	2	2	4	19	5		32
1949	–	4	5	20	3		32
1950	I	5	3	14	9		32
1951	I	3	7	20	10		41
1952	–	I	4	22	4		31
1953	I	I	I	24	7		34
1954	–	2	5	19	10		36
1955	–	–	3	14	9		26
1956	–	2	4	19	15		40
1957	–	–	2	17	8		27
1958	I	I	2	16	11		31
1959	–	I	5	17	7		30
1960	–	–	7	11	12		30
1961	–	I	I	12	12		26
1962	–	I	5	21	7		34
1963	–	I	5	16	8		30
1964	I	I	3	15	6		26
1965	–	–	2	14	11		27
1966	–	2	3	16	8		29
1967	I	–	6	12	4		23
Total	19	76	152	567	271		1,085

Table 11 Deaths – Where People Died

	At Home	In Hospital	Total
1933	24	2	26
1934	21	6	27
1935	28	5	33
1936	30	7	37
1937	32	4	36
1938	24	3	27
1939	19	4	23
1940	23	8	31
1941	25	4	29
1942	28	4	32
1943	31	9	40
1944	39	8	47
1945	21	9	30
1946	22	4	26
1947	22	2	24
1948	30	2	32
1949	25	7	32
1950	27	5	32
1951	25	16	41
1952	23	8	31
1953	25	9	34
1954	23	13	36
1955	18	8	26
1956	19	21	40
1957	17	10	27
1958	23	8	31
1959	18	12	30
1960	20	10	30
1961	14	12	26
1962	17	17	34
1963	19	11	30
1964	18	8	26
1965	16	11	27
1966	17	12	29
1967	13	10	23
Totals	796	289	1,085

younger groups. Over the entire period, 796 persons, or 73 per cent of the total deaths, died at home, 289 persons, or 27 per cent, died in a variety of hospitals or institutions (Table 11). At the beginning of the period comparatively few died away from home, only two out of twenty-six in the year 1933. By 1966, however, this proportion had changed to nine out of twenty-three. This change, like the change in baptismal practice, had economic implications. 'Incidentally, the growing practice of doctors sending very many of their patients to hospital and their dying there after a month has seriously affected revenue in the home parishes as a quarter of the funeral offerings is diverted – fourteen of ours died in Longford and two in Mullingar in 1951.'[8] The arrangement here referred to was a local statute that directed that the clergy of the parish in which the hospital or home was situated would be given a quarter of the Funeral Offerings to reimburse them for their chaplaincy work in the hospital or home, if the patient resided there for a month or more. When this began to happen frequently revenue in the home parishes decreased sharply.

The depression and lack of confidence in the future that characterised this period is best illustrated by comparing the small number of marriages that took place at home with the much larger number that took place among those who emigrated. Obviously, even a modest improvement in their circumstances gave many of those who left the security to marry – sometimes quite soon after their departure. Indeed, emigration – its causes and effects – is a dominant theme in the life of the parish during all these years. It ensured that, though the birth-rate was high, the population was continually declining. It caused anxiety to the parish clergy as to whether those who were leaving were aequately prepared, whether they were sufficiently mature and instructed in their religious beliefs to withstand the 'culture-shock' and to handle their new-found freedom. It shaped many of the catechetical initiatives that were undertaken. It deprived the parish of the brightest and most ambitious of its children. Other changes, too, were impacting on the life of the parish – more children were being born in hospitals and nursing-homes – so more baptisms took place outside the parish. Increasingly too, hospitals and nursing-homes were the places where parishioners died and this changed the role of the parish clergy in the pastoral care of the sick. In spite of all these changes and challenges, efforts continued to improve the quality of parish ministration and to strengthen and encourage parishioners in their resolve to survive.

Patterns of Religious Practice
(The 1939 Survey)

We kept this year a record of the numbers who attended Holy Mass, received Holy Communion and came to Evening Devotions during the year on Sundays and weekdays – and next page gives particulars.[1,2]

THE PARISH REGIME: AN OVERVIEW

The Catholic population of the parish in 1939 was 2,529 and the number of households was 540.[3] These people were served by three priests – the parish priest, Canon Dennis O'Kane, and two curates, Fr Thomas D. Sheeran and Fr Patrick McCormaic. There were two churches – St Mary's parish church, built between 1860 and 1867 and St Guasacht's,[4] one mile west of the modern town of Granard. It had been the parish church from about 1830 (according to tradition) until 1867 and was retained as a 'chapel of ease' until 1961 when it was de-commissioned and demolished.[5] St Mary's occupied a commanding position on the hill but this very position caused great difficulty 'for the old and infirm find it a big tax on their strength to climb the hill'.[6]

From the church notice-books, preserved in the parish archive (covering the period 1908 to the present), it is possible to deduce the regime of church ceremonies and the range of services offered. There were three public masses each Sunday, at 8 a.m. and 11 a.m. in St Mary's and at 9.30 a.m. in St Guasacht's. (Mass was also celebrated daily in the convent chapel for the Mercy Sisters at 7.30 a.m.). Mass was celebrated in St Mary's each week-morning at 8 a.m. The three priests were available for confession each Saturday from 12 noon to 2 p.m. and from 7 p.m. until 9 p.m. They were similarly available on the eves of Holydays and, on the Thursday previous to the First Friday, they were available from 7 p.m. to 9 p.m. The arrangements for masses on Holydays was the same as that for Sundays.

The first Sunday of the month was assigned to the Sodality of the Sacred Heart (men and women). This one was not so highly organised as the Sodality of the Immaculate Conception, which had a men's and a women's branch both of which held regular monthly meetings, but it had a certain loyal following. The second Sunday was general communion day for the women's branch of the Sodality of the Immaculate Conception.

The third Sunday was general communion day for the men's branch of the same Sodality and the fourth Sunday was general communion day for the children of primary school age and for those recently finished primary school, who formed the catechism class which was held each Sunday after 11 a.m. mass in St Mary's Church. In each case what was expected was that the members of the designated group would go to confession on the Saturday and receive Holy Communion at 8 a.m. mass on Sunday.

As a general rule, there was a holy hour (an hour's prayer, partly private, partly community) in the Church and in the presence of the Blessed Sacrament) on the first Sunday of each month at 7p.m. This was attended by the members of the Sacred Heart Sodality though not exclusively by them. There was always one of the priests present to lead this hour's prayer. On the second Sunday, at the same hour, there was a meeting of the women's branch of the Sodality of the Immaculate Conception[7] and on the third Sunday a meeting of the men's branch. Each of these meetings had one of the priests in attendance and it took the form of prayer (usually the rosary) a fairly lengthy sermon or instruction and benediction of the Most Blessed Sacrament. The meeting, under the direction of the prefects of the Sodality, also transacted whatever business was proper to, or required for, its continued working. On the fourth Sunday there were evening devotions open to all (again rosary, sermon and benediction formed the core) with the members of the Legion of Mary especially invited to be involved. Another sodality, called the Children of Mary, also existed. It was primarily but not exclusively, aimed at young girls in their teens and up to the time of their marriage. It was based in the Convent of Mercy, where members met after the 11 a.m. mass on the third and fourth Sundays of the month. It, too, had the assistance of one of the priests as spiritual director. It aimed to provide adult religious education and faith formation. It operated a lending library for the use and benefit of its members.[8] Evening devotions were organised every evening except Saturday evening during Lent – the emphasis here being on self-denial and penance and particularly on the Way of the Cross – and every evening except Saturday during May, when devotion to the Blessed Virgin Mary was cultivated. This programme was developed gradually from the beginning of the century. It had taken definite form by the mid 1920s and was consolidated in the period under review.

Against the background of this programme it is possible to interpret the information contained in Appendix 1. It must be remembered, however, that this has one defect. It does not include the numbers who shared in the celebration of mass in St Guasacht's, Granardkille, each Sunday at 9.30 a.m. We know that the seating capacity of this church, with its three galleries, was about 300 people. We need to remember to include a notional figure for this in our calculations.

PATTERNS OF MASS-ATTENDANCE

Attendance at Sunday mass was regarded as obligatory on all Catholics from school going age until old-age or infirmity made it no longer possible. However, factors like personal illness, distance from the church, weather conditions, modes of or lack of transport, even economic circumstances (too poor to afford decent clothing) were regarded as valid excuses for non-attendance occasionally or even habitually. There is some circumstantial evidence that there was a pastoral problem in relation to mass-attendance in Granard parish during the nineteenth and twentieth centuries.[9] The bad practices which developed when there was insufficient room in Granardkille church seem to have died slowly. Appendix 1 reveals an average Sunday mass attendance over the year 1939 of 1,148. If we allow a further 250 or so for Granardkille, the average becomes 1,400 people out of a population of 2,529, or 55.4 per cent.

We do not have an age break-down of the population for that year, but it is unlikely that a 45 per cent absence could be accounted for by including pre-school children, the sick and those of advanced age. Poverty could certainly have played a part and the location of the church, making access and egress difficult, particularly in wintertime, certainly contributed to what was, undoubtedly a lower than average mass-attendance. Those on the fringes of the parish may have gone to mass in neighbouring churches at Clonbroney, Purth or Carra and there would not have been any compensation from these parishes; but there still appears to have been a hard core who stayed away in spite of the frequent and forthright admonitions of parish clergy and bishop.[10]

When the monthly averages are examined they show a fluctuation over the year from a low of 971 in December to a high of 1,241 in March – a variation of 21.7 per cent. The average for the winter months, November, December, January and February, is 1,017; while the average over the summer months, May, June, July and August is 1,203 – a variation of 15.5 per cent. Weather conditions, difficulty of reaching the Church (especially for old or weak people) and seasonal illnesses probably account for these results. Significantly, the highest average attendances are recorded for the months of March and April – the period of Lent and Eastertide.[11] This would indicate that the emphasis on Lent and Eastertide as the high season of the liturgical year was having some effect. Table 12 sets out monthly averages for Sunday mass attendance in St Mary's church for 1939 in descending order.

The weekday mass attendance was not generally high and actually fell as low as twelve in mid-January, 1939, but it rose sharply during Lent, averaging 202 per day over the forty days. It was also high in May when the daily average was 110 and in October when it reached 106.

Table 12 St Mary's Church, Average Attendances at Sunday Mass, 1939

March	1,241	October	1,224	November	1,082
April	1,234	September	1,195	February	1,034
July	1,231	June	1,178	January	981
August	1,228	May	1,173	December	971

PATTERNS OF RECEPTION OF HOLY COMMUNION

The first and most obvious inference from Appendix 1 is that those who received holy communion invariably did so at the earlier mass at 8 a.m. Quite astonishingly, in the light of present-day thinking, the sacrament was not shared and was received only by the priest-celebrant at the later mass. This of course, was a product of the church discipline which required all communicants – priest and laity – to observe the 'Eucharistic fast'. This meant that they took neither food nor drink from the previous midnight. Therefore, people went to the earliest available mass when they wished to receive communion. This would be especially the case with the rural community where a certain amount of work would always have to be done – even on Sundays. The second inference is that the numbers receiving holy communion were relatively small. On the first day of the New Year (1939), for example, out of a total of 1,009 who attended Mass only 180 (or 17.8 per cent) received holy communion. The highest number of communicants in the month of January that year was 480 and this was recorded on the fourth Sunday of the month which was general communion day for children. The third and fourth Sundays of each month – the general communion days for men and children – show the highest and most consistent numbers of communicants. The women – who had their general communion day on the second Sunday of each month – seem to have divided their attention between that Sunday and the first Friday of the month.[12] The numbers of communicants were highest on Christmas Day (395 or 65 per cent of total attendance) and Easter Sunday (369 or 55 per cent of total attendance). Only thirty-one per cent of total attendance received holy communion on Trinity Sunday. This could be considered remarkable as there was ususally a rush on this occasion to fulfill the 'Easter duty'. The church notice-book provides evidence that attention was drawn to this fact two weeks earlier.[13] The numbers who received holy communion on week days formed a higher proportion of total attendance reaching a high of 188 out of 240 or seventy-eight per cent on 5 May 1939. This is explained by the fact that, as a general rule, only the more deeply committed would be regularly attending week-day mass.

THE ROLE OF SODALITIES AND POPULAR DEVOTIONS

An analysis of the church notice-books reveals that sodality general communion days, sodality meetings, holy hours and certain other devotions
formed an integral part of the Catholic life of the parish. The essential
feature of 'Sodalities' or 'Pious Association' was the support of the members for one another and the encouragement and good example which
each received from the group.[14] A secondary feature was the potential
these highly organised and motivated groups had for spiritual formation.
As well as ensuring that they themselves practised their religion regularly
their membership of the sodality enhanced their knowledge of Catholic
doctrine and provided an opportunity for them to be formed as lay apostles. Sodality members were expected to set a high standard of behaviour
and of religious practice and to assume leadership roles in the Catholic
community. Their prefects were given positions of responsibility and of
honour in various church functions especially in the Corpus Christi procession.[15] Not all parishioners, of course, were members of sodalities. The
spiritual needs of these individuals were addressed through popular devotions related more to fostering piety than to the intellectual formation
and were less highly organised, less regimented and more occasional in
character. Such, for instance, were the Marian Devotions in May and
October.

The various levels of involvement and the emphasis placed when
addressing each group can be illustrated from the texts of two surviving
addresses of Fr Donal O'Lehane, who was a curate in the parish from
1948 to 1960. He was, perhaps, the outstanding preacher of that period
with a particular interest in and wish to communicate the social teaching
of the Catholic church. An address, delivered to the monthly meeting of
the men's branch of the Sodality of the Immaculate Conception in May
1951, treats of the subject of the family. It was a powerful intellectual
exposition of the meaning of family, the role of parents, the place of children and the rights of family vis-a-vis the state. It was obviously intended
for those who had a reasonable standard of education, an ability to deal
with abstract concepts and a more than average level of interest in church
teaching. The complete text is printed as appendix two to this study. A
month earlier he had given a holy hour on the Sunday after Easter
Sunday. The emphasis here was reflective and prayerful rather then didac-
tic. It focused first on the Gospel reading of the day (Jn. 20:19-31) to
emphasise faith and peace through the sacrament of penance. It then drew
attention to the fate of the disciples on the road to Emmaus (Lk. 20:13-35)
to suggest courage and hope renewed (appendix three).

There were, of course, those who remained uninvolved at either level
– the minimalists, who came to church late and left early and those who

came infrequently or not at all. The great effort to reach these was made through the parish mission. Canon O'Kane inherited a situation whereby a parish mission, lasting one week, was held annually. From the beginning he had doubts about the efficacy of such an arrangement[16] but it was only in 1938 that a definite decision was made to attempt a greater effort at longer intervals in the hope of achieving better long-term results. In that year the Capuchins preached the mission and at the end of it the leader of the team, Fr Columbus, gave 'his impressions and his advice'.

> He says we are a bad lot indeed ... He strongly recommended that in future we should, if possible, have a two week mission (not necessarily every year), one for women and one for men, – with the first day for children and a special appeal to them to make themselves unusually useful for the rest of the mission so as to release and send their parents every evening. Further, no priests should be invited to assist at the confessions. The two Mission Fathers should hear all – warning off people from other parishes, if necessary. These two men should have an agreed programme and plan to waken up the hardy-annuals, the *consuetudinarii*, the *recidivi* and the *occasionarii*, these latter especially. We have very bad customs and practices to eradicate, a very low moral standard to elevate, a very pagan and material outlook to confound, and *de sexto et nono* a revolution to accomplish. Separate instruction in pulpit and strict individual treatment in the confessional should effect an improvement. The present method is not sufficient for the needs of the place.[17]

Up to 1938 there was a one-week parish mission each year: from 1940 there was a two-week mission every three years. Over the entire period sixteen parish missions were preached – six by Redemptorists, three by Capuchins, two each by Passionists, Oblates and House of Missions Fathers and one by Augustinians. In spite of all this effort the problems of carelessness and indifference were never quite eradicated. So in 1946 'there was a very good attendance generally morning and evening, and, as usual, great enthusiasm while the Mission lasted; but, alas for the instability of human nature, the good resolutions seemed to have been dissipated soon by the cares and pleasures of the world'.[18]

In a typical month the first Sunday would have an evening holy hour from 7 p.m. to 8 p.m. It would be general in its appeal, would include the rosary usually with some reflection on each mystery, a number of prayers of adoration, thanksgiving and petition, periods of silent reflection for personal prayer and, to conclude, the benediction (or blessing of the congregation with the Sacred Host displayed in the monstrance). The order and pattern, except for the benediction, might vary with the time of year or in

response to a particular need or circumstance, like the need for fine
weather to save the crops or the threatening catastrophe of the second
world war.[19] The second and third Sundays would be the general communion days consecutively for women and men members of the Sodality of
the Immaculate Conception. Monthly confession on the Saturday formed
part of the preparation for this general communion. On the evening of
the Sunday of their general communion women or men met in church at
7 p.m. for an hour-long gathering consisting of prayer, instruction, discussion and concluding with benediction. On the fourth Sunday people
gathered for evening devotions – again popular prayers and hymns, a short
instruction or reflection and benediction. The appeal was to a general
audience but often some parish group like the Legion of Mary was asked
to take a leading part. In Lent evening devotions took place each evening
of the week except Saturday evening (when the priests were engaged in
hearing confessions). At this time the Way of the Cross and other prayers
focusing on the passion of Christ formed the core of these devotions. In
May and October, when again evening devotions were organised each
evening except Saturday, the emphasis was on devotion to Our Lady
under her various titles, with the fifteen mysteries of the rosary and several
acts of consecration providing the framework and the themes. Except for
the 'peer pressure' exerted on members of the sodality in relation to their
monthly meeting, attendance at any of these evening services was entirely
voluntary. Accordingly, the considerable numbers of people who came to
take part must have had a high degree of spiritual motivation. Later,
cynics were to suggest that they went for want of anything else to do or
to get away from home or to meet people coming or going.[20]

Appendix 1 is not entirely satisfactory in so far as it does not provide
figures for attendance at the various evening devotions for the month of
January and part of February – in fact, until the beginning of Lent. From
the church notice-book, however, we know that all the usual meetings
and devotions did take place during these months, so we may safely
assume that the numbers who attended (with, perhaps, some small seasonal variation) were on a par with those of the other months. The average
attendance each evening during Lent was 247. This was a significant figure
and suggests that there was a sizeable group of people who took the
Catholic church's long period of preparation for the celebration of Holy
Week and Easter sufficiently seriously to make the journey to the church
each day for public community prayer and reflection. It also indicates that
the parish priest and his assistants were dedicated and successful in their
pastoral leadership with a substantial minority of parishioners.

'In St Mary's Church the greater feasts of the Mother of God are celebrated with special solemnity …'[21] Figures from Appendix 1 serve to illustrate that not just individual feasts days but also times of the year when

Marian devotion is highlighted in the Catholic church, namely May and October, were similarly celebrated. The average daily attendance at May devotions was 133 in spite of the fact that the onset of summer might be expected to provide rival attractions. October devotions were organised for the Sunday evenings of October only and the average attendance over the five Sundays was 140. Even in the times and seasons of the year when there was no particular devotional emphasis, in the summer season, for instance, there was remarkable fidelity to these Sunday evening devotions. The average attendance, excluding May and October, is 142. We look, finally, at Devotion to the Sacred Heart of Jesus as it expresses itself in the practice of attending mass and receiving holy communion on the first Friday of each month. The average attendance at first Friday morning mass (at 8 a.m.) over the year 1939 was 275 and the average of communicants was 188.

It is reasonable to ask how well this approach to pastoral ministry worked, but difficult in the extreme to reach precise conclusions. In general, it may be said that basic practice (nominal mass-attendance) was lower than the general average. The bad habits acquired in the years when there was not enough room in the church at Granardkille to hold the congregation were obviously transmitted. The comments of the Capuchin missioner in 1938 suggests that all the efforts at reform after the great four-week mission, preached by the Dominicans when the parish church of St Mary was opened in 1867, had been no more than partially successful. On the other hand it is equally clear that there was a consistent support from ten to twenty per cent of parishioners for every form of devotion offered. It was to that group, especially, that the clergy would have looked for loyal and effective lay leadership.

The Pioneer Total Abstinence Association, the Legion of Mary and the St Vincent de Paul Society were also established in the parish at the time of Canon O'Kane's appointment as parish priest.[22] His predecessor, Canon Patrick Donohoe, had been a very strong advocate of the PTAA and has promoted it vigorously. In spite of this the Association was not very active in 1933. In his review of the parish at the end of his first year, the new parish priest had this to say:

> There is a Pioneer Total Abstinence Sodality – the men meeting quarterly in the Church and the women in the Convent. There is a big list of names; but attendance – especially in the case of women and girls – is ridiculously small, absolutely and relatively to the number on roll. Fr Mac Cormaic took on the work of Spiritual Director, brought both sections to the Church for their meeting and, in the beginning, strove earnestly to put life into the Sodality by sifting the lists of members and finding who were in earnest and

who gave in their names at one time and never after attended a
meeting or took any interest in the Sodality.[23]

Canon O'Kane obviously treated the local branch of the association as
another sodality and expected its members to do much more than give in
their name, wear a pin, and observe the total abstinence pledge. He, and
his curate, Fr Patrick Mac Cormaic, obviously intended to emphasise the
spiritual dimesion of the Association and to use it as a vehicle for formation and education. Both were members of the Association themselves
and continued in membership to the end of their days.

The Legion of Mary, we learn, had only recently been established.
Undoubtedly, it had been established with the blessing of O'Kane's pre-
decessor, Canon Donohoe, who was also very enthusiastic about all
Marian devotions. The new parish priest was less convinced:

> There is also a branch of the Legion of Mary, not long established
> and in poor standing with the central authorities in Dublin ... A
> great many members were enrolled in the first enthusiasm, but the
> monotony of the work, the uncompromising stringency of the
> Rules and the unpleasantness of visitation caused a great falling-off
> in members. Now there are only ten or eleven active members –
> mostly elderly and rather unsuited for the class of work the Legion
> has in mind.[24]

Poverty on a fairly wide scale has been part of the environment of
Granard and the records of the Granard branch employment exchange,
which was established in 1934, show a consistently high application rate
for any available form of subvention or help. Obviously there was great
scope for an organisation like the St Vincent de Paul Society and this had
been established at least as early as 1913.[25] But the very size of the task
acted as a deterrent to those who might be expected to join, as the following comment from the annual report for 1933 suggests:

> There is a St Vincent de Paul Conference – few in numbers,
> though there was a large membership some years ago, but equal to
> the work to be done. The six or seven members attend regularly,
> carry out their visitations faithfully and live up to the spirit of the
> great organisation to which they belong. They collect at the
> Church gate during the winter months: each Christmas the Most
> Rev Bishop sends the Conference five pounds and their chief rev-
> enue is a grant, as needed, from the Murta Charity Fund.[26]

All three of these organisations continued at least to function, if not to flourish, for the next four decades. The St Vincent de Paul Conference remained numerically small. The president, it appears, thought that it was better to have even a very small number who would do the work that had to be done rather than a larger nominal membership. 'The spiritual director pleaded that more should be allowed to share in the good work, for their own spiritual benefit, even if they are not required for visitation etc. but the president is unmoved by any consideration.'[27] The structure of the Society gave no influence to the priest/spiritual director in the actual running of its affairs: he could only plead and make representations. Even the higher officials of the Society did not always prevail :

> A representative from Dublin visited and pleaded for recruitment. His attention was also called to rather indiscriminate and human benefaction at Christmas-time but on both matters he does not seem to have produced any change of attitude or practice.[28]

One cannot avoid feeling that the canon was the one who drew this to his attention. In 1949 the long-standing and strong-willed president, Mr Frank Magan, the local solicitor, died, and was succeeded by a local businessman, P.J. Brady. Five or six young members joined and all continue the good work satisfactorily.[29] From the annual report for 1961 comes the only evidence of tension arising from the work of the Society. It draws attention to the fact that expectations of a better standard of living – even among the poorer people – were beginning to rise. They saw the wide range of new consumer goods that appeared in the post-war period and, in their attempts to get these, sometimes incurred debts they could not meet and were short on the necessities of life. Canon O'Kane, now an elderly man and with very little interest in or appreciation of what he would have considered luxury-goods saw no reason for the St Vincent de Paul Society to subvent their improvidence.

> ... itinerants were given houses in St Colmcille's Terrace and they expected the St Vincent de Paul Brothers to 'carry them' whilst their Childrens' Allowances were spent on drink and rowdyism and the land and garden owners had endless trespass from their horses and goats. Similarly, our native poor considered themselves entitled to television, radio and electrical equipment, on Hire-Purchase terms, and they were agrieved when the Canon Dolan[30] and other charities were not available to meet their heavy demands for these luxuries and some of them adopted the Trades Union practice of going on strike: in this case ceasing to attend Sodalities, Christian Doctrine Instruction, Devotions and, in a few cases, even Mass for a time.[31]

As already noted, Canon O'Kane was himself a deeply committed member of the Pioneer Total Abstinence Association. He retained the pioneer pin that, as a young man, he had received from the founder of the Association, Fr Cullen.[32] A number of his curates, especially Fr MacCormaic and Fr O'Lehane were equally dedicated. Fr O'Lehane, in particular, was a powerful advocate of the Association's spirituality.[33] There was a council meeting once a month, separately for men, for women and for juveniles. There was a monthly meeting in each of the primary schools on or near the first Friday of each month for juveniles and those about to take, or having recently taken, the Confirmation pledge. There was a quarterly general meeting of all adult members – men in the church, women in the convent. There was an annual parish rally at evening devotions of all under twenty-one years with a renewal of the Confirmation pledge and Temperance Sunday was given a special high-lighting annually.[34] Though the structure was good on paper, the reality was less satisfactory. Rather surprisingly, there seems to have been more enthusiasm among the men that among the women. The annual report for 1938, referring to the quarterly general meeting says 'men again very loyal, though numbers not very large: women – rather hopeless … we had a general reunion and roll-call at the evening devotions on the fourth Sunday after Pentecost and practically all those still in the parish and under twenty-one attended'.[35] From time to time some celebrated animator was called in to put new enthusiasm into the movement. In 1955, for instance, we learn that: Fr Doherty SJ came on 9 January and spoke at all three masses and at 7.30 p.m. for children. At 8.30 p.m. there was a pioneer concert and address.[36] There was also an outing on 29 June.[37] Precise numbers are difficult to establish because of the loss or destruction in recent years of the centre's registers, but enquiries made locally suggest that the combined membership never went above one hundred and fifty adult members and, as the annual reports suggest, not all of these were active. In the annual report for 1953 Canon O'Kane reflected on the causes of defection from the Association.

> It is distressing, but, I suppose, inevitable that some young men break off when they get old enough to travel around and the strong canvass and the bad example of new companions prove too much for them. Football clubs, farmers' organisations, coursing, dancing, excursions, finals in Croke Park all provide occasions for outings and for indulgence. In most cases, too, it is the very men who should not that do begin drinking (and where will they end!), because their former history in this regard is not encouraging … [38]

The poor relation among these organisations seems to have been the

Legion of Mary. The doubts about its potential expressed in the annual report for 1933 (as already mentioned) seem to have lingered. Three years later, for example, we are told: 'the Legion of Mary struggled on, with reduced membership (some old, some infirm and no recruits coming in ... Many appeals and canvassings brought only very poor results – until October, when all the officers of the Legion agreed to resign their official positons (but to continue as ordinary members) and four new recruits were appointed – president, vice-president, treasurer and secretary – and a few other new members joined ... and we hope, at least, to have some life and business in this organisation'.[39] In 1949 it was reported that: the Legion of Mary carried on without much demonstration, but is is hard to keep up numbers of active members.[40] In 1953, in an attempt to strength-en its impact, four Dublin legionaries came during their summer holidays and visited all the local *praesidia* and did routine visitation with the local members. Their zeal, the fact they sacrificed part of their holidays, their experience and their methods benefitted the Granard legionaries greatly. This, together with a change of officers and some new members, brought about a revitalisation for a while.[41]

The most significant contribution of the Legion of Mary in Granard was the introduction, in 1957, of Patrician meetings. The parish priest quickly identified one important advantage of this – it got people to dis-cuss religion and religious topics.[42] It raised difficulties when the subject of labour relations surfaced – employees were aggressive and employers reluctant to take part – and it revealed an attitude to work among the young which horrified the parish priest: it is drudgery and slavery and the less of it one can get off with the better: hold on to some sort of job for thirteen weeks and then draw 'dole' or stamps for six months is the motto.[43] Despite these difficulties and disedifying revelations Patrician meetings continued to be organised and the memory of some of them, when Fr Donal O'Lehane was spiritual director, is still vivid with those who took part.[44]

The statistics on which this chapter is based give a unique and fascinat-ing insight into the Catholic life of the parish in the eventful year of 1939. They reveal a parish that was well served with opportunities for worship, prayer and spiritual and personal development. They reveal, too, a parish which had a core of staunch, loyal supporters; but they also draw attention to the fact that there was a large number who were less than dedicated and only nominally involved with mainstream parochial life. It is clear that the parish priest and his curates were aware of this situtaiton and attempt-ed to redress it with a variety of strategies. They placed great emphasis on preaching and on catechetical instruction. They encouraged the formation of sodalities to provide opportunities for adult education and organised parish missions to encourage renewal of religious fervour. They attempted to identify and to counter specific abuses. They were high in their hopes, but realistic in their expectations. They set high standards and, if these were not always reached, they continued undeterred.

Conclusion

We have looked at a phase in the life of a relatively small Catholic community in north county Longford – half town, half country – economically underdeveloped, fighting a losing battle to retain its population, showing symptoms of the alienation that regularly accompanies poverty and deprivation, yet, on the whole, well organised, well served, in large part practising and with a core of highly-motivated, highly committed and loyal parishioners.

From the population statistics the slow but steady decline in numbers emerges and the countryside is seen to suffer greater losses than the town. The figures for marriages, too, indicate that there was a palpable lack of confidence in the future and an air of acceptance that, in the depressed economic climate, the possibility of marrying and raising a family with any reasonable standard of living was often remote. Despite this, there is evidence of a great sense of loyalty both to the parish and to the priests who served it. There is evidence in the income and expenditure figures of a general willingness to provide for the basic essentials, but there is also evidence that necessary capital expenditure posed a serious problem both for the parish priest, because he was aware of the inconvenience that his necessary fund-raising would cause, and for the people, since many families found the request even for £10 burdensome. When confronted with the task of raising £3,000 or more in 1940, this is how he set about his appeal. At each meeting:

> I put it to them this way: we have approximately five hundred families in this parish. Of these about two hundred occupy labourers' cottages or urban council houses – these could contribute only very little. If the remaining three hundred families contributed £10 each, the total would be £3,000. But of course many of the three hundred had only small holdings and could not subscribe £10; so that, to secure an average of £10, those better off would have to give £20, £15 etc. I said I did not like a 'cess' and a flat rate taxation: rate collectors are not popular! I rather hoped that people would support this good work according to their means remembering that it was to God they were giving it ...[1]

According to the calculations used converting income and expenditure to contain contemporary values £10 in 1940 would be the equivalent of nearly £500 in 1995. The generosity of the community to its priests is obvious in the level of contribution made to their upkeep: when expressed in today's values it is shown to be higher than contemporary provision, not withstanding the economic advances of the past thirty years.

When examined in detail, through Table 5, the level of involvement of the parish priest and his various curates with the people of the parish is impressive. They shared the joy of welcoming more than seventeen hundred new members into the congregation – all but two of them as infants. They assisted at the funerals of more than a thousand people – thus ministering to almost every family in the parish on more than one occasion at a time when the bereaved family would have been at its most vulnerable. They would also, of course, have assisted all those who died at home with the sacraments of penance, eucharist, and last anointing. The Sick-Call Book, covering the years 1921 to 1945, records a total of sixty-one sick calls for the year 1939. They were acutely aware of the threat to the vitality of the parish community occasioned by the low marriage rate and bemoaned it not just because they themselves might suffer some material disadvantage because of it. They helped to prepare more than seventeen hundred children and young people for confirmation in the full knowledge that many of these were going to live their lives away from their own parish and country and were probably not going to get a great deal more in the way of formal religious instruction.

Finally, we see a community well provided for with opportunities both of liturgical and of popular devotion and, while the response was satisfactory – even impressive – in many ways, one can deduce that the parish was by no means problem-free. There certainly was a serious deficit in basic practice (mass-attendance) though the precise extent is impossible to quantify. Though the movement towards more frequent reception of Holy Communion had been underway in the church since the early part of the century, it seems to have been no more than partially successful in the parish of Granard as the mid-century approached. On the other hand, there is evidence of a vibrant prayer-life among a sizeable number of parishioners. The rosary was, here as elsewhere, the most commonly practised form of community prayer, with the Way of the Cross also commanding wide appeal. Eucharistic devotion – prayer before the Blessed Sacrament and the Blessing of the Congregation with the Holy Eucharist (Benediction) were a regular feature of the life of the devout and marked almost every occasion of special devotion or celebration in the parish. Much valuable information about the life and circumstances of the parish has been gleaned from a study of the figures left behind by a careful administrator and the leader of an energetic pastoral team.

There was much to celebrate and much to bemoan in the workload of Canon O'Kane and the various curates who assisted him in his long pastorate. In joy and in sorrow, in success or in failure, welcome or unwelcome, he and they remained involved. Indeed, involvement must be the one single word that would describe the findings of this study – involvement at every level of the life of the parish and of its people. In the annual report for 1959 (now in the autumn of his pastorate) he summed up the nature and extent of this involvement and, almost unwittingly, defined its priorities.

It occured to me to catalogue sometime (as a matter of interest or curiosity) some of the activities and preoccupations of the clergy (chiefly the indefatigable curates) – apart from their essential duties of masses, confessions, devotions, baptisms, sick-calls, funerals:

1. St Vincent de Paul Society – meeting once a week and many visitations personally on this work.
2. The Legion of Mary – *Praesidium* meeting one for men and one for women each week: a *Curia* meeting once a month with Acies and rallies occasionally.
3. Patrician meeting – once a month – one for men, one for women, one for boys.
4. Children of Mary (girls and women) – twice a month – with an annual retreat and processions and functions.
5. Pioneer Total Abstinence Meetings – a big tax on time – council meetings once a month separately for men, for women and for families: once a month in each of the national schools, on or near the first Friday for juveniles and confirmation pledges: Temperance Sunday: parish rally at evening devotions for all under twenty-one and renewal of Confirmation pledges: every quarter a general meeting of pioneers – men in the church, women in the convent national school.
6. National schools – Christian doctrine every day in one or other of the five schools.
7. Convent secondary school – three classes each week.
8. Vocational school – four classes each week – two for boys and two for girls – and a special course of four talks on social science for the Young Farmers' winter classes.
9. Choir-practices: Mass-servers' instructions: Holy Week preparation: carol-singing.
10. Almost every week-morning the sacraments are brought to the old and sick in their homes in the country districts and, on each first Friday morning, to those in the town.

11. After the closing of convent and boys' schools the priests gave a detailed and visual demonstration of all the ceremonies of the mass and in these and the other schools practised the dialogue mass, ending with active participation at the 9.30a.m. public mass every Sunday. (May God hasten the day when the vernacular will be permitted in the liturgy generally – including the Divine Office!).

12. Time was also found for attending meetings and exploring the possibility of starting some industry in the town and acquiring a town park, for running a mens' and boys' club in Moxham Street hall, for training a dramatic group, for encouraging various football teams etc.[2]

At the beginning of Canon O'Kane's pastorate he was a citizen of the Irish Free State: by the time of his death he was a citizen of the Irish Republic. At the beginning there was a confidence in the Irish Catholic Church that smacked of triumphalism, almost at times of arrogance, while there was still considerable uncertainty about the future of the fledgling state. By the time of his death the new Republic had gained in confidence to the extent that it was turning its attention towards the emerging EEC (later to become the EC and most recently the EU), while in the Catholic Church the winds of change had begun to blow – old certainties were about to be, or were already being, challenged and service, not dominance, had become the buzz-word. Even his exit seemed appropriately timed. The old order was changing – yielding place to the new.

Appendices

Statistics of Church Attendance during 1939

JANUARY

	Sun	Mon	Tue	Wed	Thu	Fri[1]	Sat	Week 1
Mass 1	309	32	27	12	19	319[2]	25	1
Hy Comm	180	18	14	3	11	140	13	to
Mass 2	700	-	-	-	-	625	7	7
Eve Dev	-	-	-	-	-	-	-	

	Sun	Mon	Tue	Wed	Thu	Fri	Sat	Week 2
Mass 1	305	31	32	27	23	19	25	8
Hy Comm	131	14	14	12	8	10	15	to
Mass 2	583	-	-	-	-	-	-	14
Eve Dev	-	-	-	-	-	-	-	

	Sun	Mon	Tue	Wed	Thu	Fri	Sat	Week 3
Mass 1	426	27	41	36	43	34	48	15
Hy Comm	137	10	12	12	10	8	26	to
Mass 2	686	-	-	-	-	-	-	21
Eve Dev	-	-	-	-	-	-	-	

	Sun	Mon	Tue	Wed	Thu	Fri	Sat	Week 4
Mass 1	407	31	30	24	16	7	32	22
Hy Comm	292	15	16	9	6	4	21	to
Mass 2	480	-	-	-	-	-	-	28
Eve Dev	-	-	-	-	-	-	-	

	Sun	Mon	Tue	Wed	Thu	Fri	Sat	Week 5
Mass 1	268	15	23					29
Hy Comm	55	5	10					to 31
Mass 2	640	-	-					to 4 Feb
Eve Dev	-	-	-					

FEBRUARY

	Sun	Mon	Tue	Wed	Thu	Fri[3]	Sat	Week 5
Mass 1				41	50	193	35	29 Jan
Hy Comm	-	-	-	7	9	150	22	to
Mass 2	-	-	-	-	-	-	-	4 Feb
Eve Dev	-	-	-	-	-	-	-	

	Sun	Mon	Tue	Wed	Thu	Fri	Sat	Week 6
Mass 1	347	78	35	43	91	40	98	5
Hy Comm	121	28	10	7	9	8	53	to
Mass 2	630	-	-	-	-	-	-	11
Eve Dev	-	-	-	-	-	-	-	

	Sun	Mon	Tue	Wed	Thu	Fri	Sat	Week 7
Mass 1	421	47	51	45	39	34	38	12
Hy Comm	148	21	16	8	7	9	14	to
Mass 2	585	-	-	-	-	-	-	18
Eve Dev	-	-	-	-	-	-	-	

	Sun	Mon	Tue	Wed[4]	Thu	Fri	Sat	Week 8
Mass 1	504	41	38	473	257	245	220	19
Hy Comm	272	13	12	16	13	11	16	to
Mass 2	576	-	-	-	-	-	-	25
Eve Dev	-	-	-	280	280	353	-	

	Sun	Mon	Tue	Wed	Thu	Fri	Sat	Week 9
Mass 1	481	198	144					26
Hy Comm	232	40	24					to 28
Mass 2	593	-	-					to 4 Mar.
Eve Dev	283	270	215					

MARCH

	Sun	Mon	Tue	Wed	Thu	Fri[5]	Sat	Week 10
Mass 1				154	183	400	162	26 Feb
Hy Comm	-	-	-	24	25	205	52	to
Mass 2	-	-	-	-	-	-	-	4 Mar
Eve Dev	-	-	-	235	248	257	-	

	Sun	Mon	Tue	Wed	Thu	Fri	Sat	Week 10
Mass 1	488	185	200	144	162	180	101	5
Hy Comm	138	35	27	17	20	19	24	to
Mass 2	608	-	-	-	-	-	-	11
Eve Dev	293	234	243	256	255	347	208	

	Sun	Mon	Tue	Wed	Thu	Fri[6]	Sat	Week 11
Mass 1	530	201	158	198	173	624	96	12
Hy Comm	170	42	28	24	33	203	33	to
Mass 2	821	-	-	-	-	278	-	18
Eve Dev	315	292	269	215	225	278	-	

	Sun	Mon	Tue	Wed	Thu	Fri	Sat	Week 12
Mass 1	504	184	147	127	128	124	143	19
Hy Comm	257	49	19	17	11	11	31	to
Mass 2	700	-	-	-	-	-	-	25
Eve Dev	303	157	181	183	175	173	-	

	Sun	Mon	Tue	Wed	Thu	Fri	Sat	Week 13
Mass 1	678	147	149	157	132	137		26
Hy Comm	241	41	39	24	19	27		to 31
Mass 2	834	-	-	-	-	-		to 1 April
Eve Dev	252	170	168	193	162	171		

APRIL

	Sun	Mon	Tue	Wed	Thu	Fri	Sat	Week 13
Mass 1							120	26 Mar
Hy Comm	-	-	-	-	-	-	40	to 1 Apr.
Mass 2	-	-	-	-	-	-	-	-
Eve Dev	-	-	-	-	-	-	-	

	Sun	Mon	Tue	Wed[7]	Thu[8]	Fri[9]	Sat[10]	Week 14
Mass 1	465	196	171	282	190	525	124	2
Hy Comm	106	34	27	28	0	0	40	to
Mass 2	718	-	-	-	-	-	-	8
Eve Dev	334	170	193	215	464	354	-	
	Sun	Mon	Tue	Wed	Thu	Fri	Sat	Week 15
Mass 1	674[11]	64	62	59	54	76	48	9
Hy Comm	369	31	21	13	7	9	30	to
Mass 2	590	-	-	-	-	-	-	15
Eve Dev	-	-	-	-	-	-	-	
	Sun	Mon	Tue	Wed	Thu	Fri	Sat	Week 16
Mass 1	596	64	62	59	54	76	48	16
Hy Comm	243	15	19	17	11	8	36	to
Mass 2	624	-	-	-	-	-	-	22
Eve Dev	-	-	-	-	-	-	-	
	Sun	Mon	Tue	Wed	Thu	Fri	Sat	Week 17
Mass 1	484	78	80	104	74	73	86	23
Hy Comm	202	24	16	18	18	13	17	to
Mass 2	743	-	-	-	-	-	-	29
Eve Dev	111	-	-	-	-	-	-	
	Sun	Mon	Tue	Wed	Thu	Fri	Sat	Week 18
Mass 1	475	-	-	-	-	-	-	30 Apr.
Hy Comm	69	-	-	-	-	-	-	to
Mass 2	802	-	-	-	-	-	-	6 May.
Eve Dev	104	-	-	-	-	-	-	

MAY

	Sun	Mon	Tue	Wed	Thu	Fri	Sat	Week 18
Mass 1		87	96	174	95	240	86	30 Apr.
Hy Comm	-	19	15	101	19	188	47	to
Mass 2	-	-	-	-	-	-	-	6 May.
Eve Dev	-	163	180	152	143	139	-	
	Sun	Mon	Tue	Wed	Thu	Fri	Sat	Week 19
Mass 1	486	111	71	75	85	95	91	7
Hy Comm	125	29	21	17	13	14	25	to
Mass 2	680	-	-	-	-	-	-	13
Eve Dev	242	152	167	133	130	123	-	
	Sun	Mon	Tue	Wed	Thu[12]	Fri	Sat	Week 20
Mass 1	485	100	102	195	428	70	64	14
Hy Comm	115	24	23	21	86	28	25	to
Mass 2	659	-	-	-	?	-	-	20
Eve Dev	170	111	148	135	-	63	-	
	Sun	Mon	Tue	Wed	Thu	Fri	Sat	Week 21
Mass 1	507	95	85	78	74	75	104	21
Hy Comm	265	25	15	13	12	14	25	to
Mass 2	720	-	-	-	-	-	-	27
Eve Dev	182	96	130	107	92	94	-	
	Sun	Mon	Tue	Wed	Thu	Fri	Sat	Week 22
Mass 1	563	84	102	96				28
Hy Comm	252	24	14	12				to 31
Mass 2	590	-	-	-				to 3 June
Eve Dev	132	86	88	94				

JUNE

	Sun	Mon	Tue	Wed	Thu	Fri[13]	Sat	Week 22
Mass 1					84	225	210	28 May
Hy Comm	-	-	-	-	12	184	98	to
Mass 2	-	-	-	-	-	-	-	3 June
Eve Dev.	-	-	-	-	-	-		

	Trinity Sun[14]	Mon	Tue	Wed	Thu[15]	Fri	Sat	Week 23
Mass 1		575	87	95	96	495	74	63 4
Hy Comm	180	20	18	18	68	19	20	to
Mass 2		550	-	-	-	547	-	-
10								
Eve Dev.	150	-	-	-	-	-	-	

	Sun	Mon	Tue	Wed	Thu	Fri[16]	Sat	Week 24
Mass 1	509	66	63	43	51	306	58	11
Hy Comm	146	21	15	12	14	88	25	to
Mass 2	684	-	-	-	-	-	-	17
Eve Dev.	-	-	-	-	-	-	-	

	Sun	Mon	Tue	Wed	Thu	Fri	Sat	Week 25
Mass 1	534	50	63	68	69	58	60	18
Hy Comm	163	22	21	18	17	17	26	to
Mass 2	619	-	-	-	-	-	-	24
Eve Dev.	93	-	-	-	-	-	-	

	Sun	Mon	Tue	Wed	Thu[17]	Fri	Sat	Week 26
Mass 1	607	58	65	61	463	57		25
Hy Comm	236	20	18	15	81	20		to
Mass 2	635	-	-	-	648	-		1 July
Eve Dev.	268	-	-	-	-	-		

JULY

	Sun	Mon	Tue	Wed	Thu	Fri	Sat	Week 27
Mass 1								65
26 June								
Hy Comm	-	-	-	-	-	-	26	to
Mass 2	-	-	-	-	-	-	-	1 July
Eve Dev.	-	-	-	-	-	-	-	

	Sun	Mon	Tue	Wed	Thu	Fri[18]	Sat	Week 28
Mass 1		400	68	64	68	64	409	68 2
Hy Comm	110	25	18	11	13	190	41	to
Mass 2	710	-	-	-	-	-	-	8
Eve Dev.	227	-	-	-	-	-	-	

	Sun	Mon	Tue	Wed	Thu	Fri	Sat	Week 28
Mass 1	509	60	70	63	61	48	68	9
Hy Comm	160	25	25	18	19	11	24	to
Mass 2	667	-	-	-	-	-	-	15
Eve Dev.	142	-	-	-	-	-	-	

	Sun	Mon	Tue	Wed	Thu	Fri	Sat	Week 29
Mass 1	563	58	62	69	66	61	54	16
Hy Comm	257	26	24	19	21	18	22	to
Mass 2	729	-	-	-	-	-	-	22
Eve Dev.	129	-	-	-	-	-	-	

	Sun	Mon	Tue	Wed	Thu	Fri	Sat	Week 30
Mass 1	610	70	64	75	71	59	50	23
Hy Comm	235	26	25	27	26	12	16	to
Mass 2	693	-	-	-	-	-	-	29
Eve Dev.	96	-	-	-	-	-	-	

	Sun	Mon	Tue	Wed	Thu	Fri	Sat	Week 31
Mass 1	500	56						30 July
Hy Comm	79	19						to
Mass 2	672	-						5 Aug.
Eve Dev.	94	-						

AUGUST

	Sun	Mon	Tue	Wed	Thu	Fri[19]	Sat	Week 31
Mass 1			60	50	66	200	76	30 July
Hy Comm	-	-	20	21	24	163	49	to
Mass 2	-	-	-	-	-	-	-	5 Aug.
Eve Dev.	-	-	-	-	-	-	-	

	Sun	Mon	Tue	Wed	Thu	Fri	Sat	Week 32
Mass 1	572	69	66	70	58	68	67	6 Aug.
Hy Comm	116	33	29	23	21	20	38	to
Mass 2	723	-	-	-	-	-	-	12.
Eve Dev.	157	-	-	-	-	-	-	

	Sun	Mon	Tue[20]	Wed	Thu	Fri	Sat	Week 33
Mass 1	553	58	530	72	63	64	67	13
Hy Comm	157	31	161	25	25	18	30	to
Mass 2	658	-	672	-	-	-	-	19
Eve Dev.	74	-	-	-	-	-	-	

	Sun	Mon	Tue	Wed	Thu	Fri	Sat	Week 34
Mass 1	570	55	60	58	57	53	62	20
Hy Comm	240	26	25	16	21	15	25	to
Mass 2	620	-	-	-	-	-	-	26
Eve Dev.	93	-	-	-	-	-	-	

	Sun	Mon	Tue	Wed	Thu	Fri	Sat	Week 35
Mass 1	588	58	70	73	73			26 Aug
Hy Comm	236	27	23	18	23			to
Mass 2	686	-	-	-	-			2 Sept.
Eve Dev.	83	-	-	-	-			

SEPTEMBER

	Sun	Mon	Tue	Wed	Thu	Fri[21]	Sat	Week 35
Mass 1						298	78	26 Aug.
Hy Comm	-	-	-	-	-	226	50	to
Mass 2	-	-	-	-	-	-	-	2 Sep.
Eve Dev.	-	-	-	-	-	-	-	

	Sun	Mon	Tue	Wed	Thu	Fri[22]	Sat	Week 36
Mass 1	525	84	87	68	96	286	146	3
Hy Comm	184	35	25	23	27	54	42	to
Mass 2	785	-	-	-	-	-	-	9
Eve Dev.	103	-	-	-	-	-	-	

	Sun	Mon	Tue	Wed	Thu	Fri	Sat	Week 37
Mass 1	488	81	85	71	72	101	69	10
Hy Comm	141	31	26	18	19	21	32	to
Mass 2	533	-	-	-	-	-	-	16
Eve Dev.	85	-	-	-	-	-		

	Sun	Mon	Tue	Wed	Thu	Fri	Sat	Week 38
Mass 1	616	71	74	76	74	88	78	17
Hy Comm	256	30	24	19	12	13	23	to
Mass 2	650	-	-	-	-	-	-	23
Eve Dev.	85	-	-	-	-	-		

	Sun	Mon	Tue	Wed	Thu	Fri	Sat	Week 39
Mass 1	572	81	90	86	87	98	80	24
Hy Comm	288	23	21	19	16	17	28	to
Mass 2	609	-	-	-	-	-	-	30.
Eve Dev.	98	-	-	-	-	-		

OCTOBER

	Sun	Mon	Tue	Wed	Thu	Fri[23]	Sat	Week 40
Mass 1	448	140	43	135	91	221	129	1
Hy Comm	96	30	30	24	15	199	63	to
Mass 2	723	-	-	-	-	-	-	7
Eve Dev.	185	-	-	-	-	-		

	Sun	Mon	Tue	Wed	Thu	Fri	Sat	Week 41
Mass 1	509	85	86	85	111	121	93	8
Hy Comm	170	38	26	19	19	18	28	to
Mass 2	663	-	-	-	-	-	-	14
Eve Dev.	125	-	-	-	-	-		

	Sun	Mon	Tue	Wed	Thu	Fri	Sat	Week 42
Mass 1	577	93	84	86	78	82	87	15
Hy Comm	259	14	19	18	17	14	38	to
Mass 2	659	-	-	-	-	-	-	21
Eve Dev.	118	-	-	-	-	-		

	Sun	Mon	Tue	Wed	Thu	Fri	Sat	Week 43
Mass 1	629	94	87	76	153	165	153	22
Hy Comm	298	29	18	18	19	21	45	to
Mass 2	764	-	-	-	-	-	-	28
Eve Dev.	126	-	-	-	-	-		

	Sun	Mon	Tue	Wed	Thu	Fri	Sat	Week 44
Mass 1	528	78	91					29
Hy Comm	173	26	32					to
Mass 2	613	-	-					4 Nov.
Eve Dev.	143	-	-					

NOVEMBER

	Sun	Mon	Tue	Wed[24]	Thu[25]	Fri[26]	Sat	Week 44
Mass 1				501	310	260	87	29 Oct
Hy Comm	-	-	-	259	164	210	49	to
Mass 2	-	-	-	603	-	-	-	4 Nov.
Eve Dev.	-	-	-	-	-	-	-	

	Sun	Mon	Tue	Wed	Thu	Fri	Sat	Week 45
Mass 1	455	81	72	76	75	77	85	5
Hy Comm	130	26	17	8	9	9	24	to
Mass 2	622	–	–	–	–	–	–	11
Eve Dev.	126	–	–	–	–	–	–	

	Sun	Mon	Tue	Wed	Thu	Fri	Sat	Week 46
Mass 1	456	84	76	84	67	68	81	12
Hy Comm	159	21	23	14	13	8	20	to
Mass 2	622	–	–	–	–	–	–	18
Eve Dev.	126	–	–	–	–	–	–	

	Sun	Mon	Tue	Wed	Thu	Fri	Sat	Week 47
Mass 1	551	86	55	60	57	54	57	19
Hy Comm	224	21	11	12	13	12	19	to
Mass 2	646	–	–	–	–	–	–	25
Eve Dev.	144	–	–	–	–	–	–	

	Sun	Mon	Tue	Wed	Thu	Fri	Sat	Week 48
Mass 1	407	60	64	59	64			26 Nov
Hy Comm	109	16	15	13	17			to
Mass 2	570	–	–	–	–			2 Dec
Eve Dev.	139	–	–	–	–			

DECEMBER

	Sun	Mon	Tue	Wed	Thu	Fri[27]	Sat	Week 48
Mass 1						260	70	26 Nov
Hy Comm	–	–	–	–	–	215	31	to
Mass 2	–	–	–	–	–	–	–	2 Dec.
Eve Dev.	–	–	–	–	–	–	–	

	Sun	Mon	Tue	Wed	Thu	Fri[28]	Sat	Week 49
Mass 1	433	66	51	56	42	425	30	3
Hy Comm	?	33	13	10	14	107	16	to
Mass 2	458	–	–	–	–	557	–	9
Eve Dev.	272	–	–	–	–	–	–	

	Sun	Mon	Tue	Wed	Thu	Fri	Sat	Week 50
Mass 1	418	43	38	38	35	36	52	10
Hy Comm	128	17	12	9	9	9	15	to
Mass 2	560	–	–	–	–	–	–	16
Eve Dev.	138	–	–	–	–	–	–	

	Sun	Mon	Tue	Wed	Thu	Fri	Sat	Week 51
Mass 1	457	45	32	38	35	48	136	17
Hy Comm	224	18	9	8	7	5	104	to
Mass 2	573	–	–	–	–	–	–	23
Eve Dev.	121	–	–	–	–	–	–	

	Sun	Mon[29]	Tue	Wed	Thu	Fri	Sat	Week 52
Mass 1	462	{421,186}	–	–	–	–	24	
Hy Comm	?	395	–	–	–	–	–	to
Mass 2	584	344	–	–	–	–	–	30
Eve Dev.	0	0	–	–	–	–	–	

APPENDIX 2

Text of an address by Fr Donal O'Lehane (who was curate in Granard from 1948 to 1960) to the monthly meeting of the men's branch of the Sodality of the Immaculate Conception in May 1951. It formed part of a series on marriage and the family. It is preserved in a manuscript note-book given to the parish archive of St Mary's, Granard after Fr O'Lehane's death as parish priest of Shannonbridge, Co. Offaly in July 1992. It is written as speaking notes.

1. Fr Lord in one of his booklets records that our popular songs tell an amazing story. There are thousands of songs about mothers – but scarcely anyone bothers to sing – much less to write – a song about Dad.

I love the dear silvery that shines in your hair – sings the tenor and the whole audience takes up the chorus of Mother Machree. Songwriters are always threatening to go back to a mother in Kentucky – in Tenessee – or in old New Hampshire. The only pieces he could rake up about father were masterpieces of mockery.

– the hat me father wore: and Everybody works but Father. He gives a possible explanation: To Dad fall the unpleasant assignments

– he must remind the children of duties they wanted to forget – of homework not done: of errands not run for mother – of toys not put properly away. His voice takes on a note of menace: I haven't noticed you doing your homework this evening. Look here, are you going to be half decent to your little sister.

2. Which reminds us of something we already know: that marriage brings into being a new society – a family. Just as God made marriage – so also God makes the family. Human Society is made up of families. The family is a society which exists prior to and indepentently of the State. Before ever there was a State – a Government – a nation – there were families. Families do not owe their existance to the state. Families have rights and duties independently of the State. The State has no authority to interfere with the family: the duty of the state is to help and assist families to carry out their task – not to take over that task and most of the duties. God instructed families to do a particular job – anyone who encroaches on the family – on the rights and duties of the family – is interfering with God's Power.

3. What is the task assigned by God to the Family.

– The Answer is – children. Into the family the child is born. Within the family the child grows up – is fed and clothed – is protected from injury and disease – is enabled to grow up into a strong healthy man or woman. Within the family too the child is trained – to use one faculty after another – to talk, to walk – to use its hands – to keep itself neat and clean – to use its mind – its conscience – to know right from wrong – to do the right, to avoid the wrong – to know God and to love Him. The task of the family is not merely to bring children into the world – but to give the world the finished article, the fully developed – properly taught and trained – young man and woman. It is the parents' right and duty and responsiblity to do all this and for this purpose God has given authority to the parents to act in his name where their children and concerned. – They hold this authority in trust from God who will demand an account of its use or abuse.

4. It is necessary for us to recall these fundamental truths and clarify our ideas about them because in our day one of the great and dangerous illusions is the conviction found among many people that all social reform and social peace can be brought about only the state intervention. So you have what they call nationalisation of industries – where the state steps in and owns the factories and produces the goods formerly produced by private enterprise. In England coal is mined by the State – the railways are owned and run as state property – Health services are administered by the state and the doctor becomes a civil servant. In Russia everything is run by the State – the very shops are state owned – the farms are taken from the owners and are worked for the state – the very lives of the people are planned for them by the State. Among other things which have suffered in all this insane grasping of power by the State is the family. The state undertakes to look after the health of the children by elaborate schemes which ignore the prior rights and duty of the father: the state undertakes to educate children without ever consulting the father's wishes as if he had no say whatever. What are we to say of all this modern tendency. Just one word: it is usurpation. The modern Government has lost its head: it has got dizzy in its desire for power and has wrongfully interfered in domains where its authority does not stand. If God wanted the State to look after his children he could have arranged it so. But God did not want that: God wanted his children looked after in the family home and to that end he gave to parents the authority and the duty of maintaining and training his little ones – an authority which he defends with a commanment all for themselves. So it is the duty of the father of the family to say to the state – Handsoff.

5. What then is the role of the State? We have it stated with authority in the words of Pius XI: the state should restrict its activity to directing, watching, stimulating, restraining, as circumstances suggest and necessity demand. In other words its function is a subsidiary – an extra one: it leaves the farmer to manage his farm – the trader to run his shop – it leaves the father to manage his family and the doctor to heal the patients – it never dares to take over the job of any one of them – but it keeps a watchful eye over them one and all providing them with facilities for doing their job. It provides schools which meet the wishes of the parents – to provide those parents with facilities for carrying out their duty of training and educating their children. It builds hospitals – staffs them with competent doctors – so that parents can have within easy reach remedies against the diseases to which their children are liable. But it leaves on the parents the duty and responsibility of paying for these services in whole or in part lest they forget whose duty it is to protect the children from disease.

6. In light of the above look at events of last week (resignation of Dr Browne, Minister for Health, 12th April 1951). How far we in Ireland are drifting from Catholic Truth? Here was a man in a responsible position – a

Catholic – approached by his Bishop who tells him that he is doing something which offiends against the teaching of his church – what does he do? Tells the bishops they are mistaken – lectures them as if they were ignorant fools – and proceeds to carry out his scheme in defiance of their wishes – which he describes as nonsense. Some friends of his held a meeting in Dublin – several speakers commence by proclaiming they are Catholics – that they accept the ruling of the bishops and then proceed to demand the carrying through of the very scheme which the Bishops condemn. Do words mean anything?. What is the use of saying one thing and doing another. If they accept the Bishops' ruling – then the scheme is gone and forget about it as good Catholics.

APPENDIX 3

Speaking notes of Fr Donal O'Lehane for a Holy Hour, which he conducted in April, 1951 on Low Sunday (i.e. the Sunday immediately following Easter Sunday.) They are reproduced with little editing.

Holy Hour April 1951. Low Sunday.

1st Quarter. Gospel of Low Sunday (Jn. 20:19-31) – narrate.

We believe in the Resurrection: Jeasus Christ – at Whose feet we are gathered tonight – died and within 3 days He shook off the grip of death – rose in glory – in victory- from the tomb. This belief involves for me many important consequences. The Gospel of First Consequence today points to one of them that I must have no more truck with sin. Why – because since He rose from the dead, He is God: being God He has authority to issue orders to me. He said – 'Go now and sin no more'- 'Be ye perfect as your Heavenly Father is perfect.' So He has given me the remedy for sin on the very day of His Ressurection – when He gave to His church the power to forgive sins – significant that He gives this power at such a time – handing to us the remedy for Sin. Are you using this divine remedy? Isn't it strange that those who need it most are the very ones who use it least and come but seldom to confession. Is it the Devil or themselves that paints the confessional as a chamber of horrors – so they became frightened and put back the remedy. He will wait till the mission: till the last week of Easter duty time. Meantime – he falls into more and more sin. He may as well sin on now – sin becomes more every day and confession menacingly difficult – This is a wrong outlook. There is joy before the angels of God over one sinners doing Penance: You have dissapointed Christ by falling into sin – but it is an added disappointment to Him to reject His mercy – His invitation to come back. After a good confession the sinner experiences a joy no words can explain. Christ strengthens with His Sacrament and helps you to keep out of sin – but remember you must keep coming. One good confession is not enough. – Keep coming. The treatment must be continued. There is nothing sacred about monthly confession – the doctor tells one patient to come back in a week – another must keep coming twice a week. A person struggling with a sin or temptation will need to come much oftener than another who is seldom tempted. We must take up in earnest the fight against sin.

2nd Quarter.

Tell story of disciples on Road to Eammaus. (Lk 24:13-35)
A second consequence: we must learn to stick close to Jesus through life. Like the disciples above we will be often discouraged. Life here is far from perfect: to keep right involves a constant struggle – often enough we will be inclined to give up and let things slide. That would be fatal – it would be inexcusable too: contrast those disciples on their road out ran the road back. Going out sad-dejected, slowly coming back – running – new hope urging them – joy in their hearts. Your sorrow shall be turned into joy – if you talk to Jesus on the way – recognise Him in the breaking of bread. He is with us in the blessed Sacraments. He didn't leave the Blessed Sacraments just for fun. He wanted to be near us and to help us on the way: abide in me: to encourage us – and we disappoint him by our neglect. – Jesus plan is – Frequent Holy Communion (he makes it so easy). Visit Him often and become intimate with him. Come to me – and I will help you. He wants our minds – to remember him often: to think of Him when in his Presence: to know Him better day by day. Our hearts – to love Him – to settle on hearts on Him and to offer Him a a wholehearted service.

Are we very casual: seldom even think of visit – go only when we have to. When there – think of anything but Him: genuflecting Him carelessly: talk to others, reject him.

– so we fail him when trials comes.

3rd Quarter. Tell Gospel story (Jn. 21:1-14 and Mt. 28:16-20)

3rd Consequence. We must hand on the good tidings to others. We must all become apostles. Christ's work in the world must be done by men – primarily by pope and priests – but every Catholic must take some of the work. When a man realises the value and the beauty of a soul and when he sees millions of those souls perishing he cannot afford to be a dog in the manger any more. A true Catholic is full of zeal for the welfare of souls – he desires to work his fingers off for souls. He will work to arouse men from their indifference – to change their hearts – We need men with the spirit of the Cure of Ars – women with the courage of Catherine Siena. The enemies of Christ are active today: even the lowest communist member is showing a zeal and activitiy that would put many Catholics to shame. He sacrifices himself for a false ideal – but we have the truth and make no effort to propagate it. Many of you are parents – to you are entrusted the lambs of Christ – Feed my Lambs – teach them – train them – make them love Jesus. Many of you could work for Christ in Vincent de Paul – in Legion of Mary – in Apostleship of Prayer. Bad spirit in Granard. No men's Praesidium of the Legion. Poor membership of Women's Branch. Children of Mary depends on county districts for membership – while town girls are too smart for that kind of thing. Even parents prevent children from delivering Catholic papers for the priest.

Where God takes possession of a soul He does not long remain inactive.

Notes

INTRODUCTION

1 James J. McNamee, *History of the diocese of Ardagh* (Dublin, 1954), p. 645.

2 Parish Returns 1993, Diocesan Archive, St Mel's, Longford.

3 For a very detailed discussion from the mid-seventeenth to the mid-nineteenth century see James Kelly, 'The Catholic Church in the diocese of Ardagh 1650-1870' in Raymond Gillespie and Gerard Moran (eds), *Longford: essays of county history* (Dublin, 1991), pp. 63-91. This paper is, incidentally, a good example of how to draw a very complete picture from quite incomplete sources.

4 Baptisms from 1779: Marriages from 1782: Deaths from 1811. Parish Archive, St Mary's, Granard, county Longford.

5 Various documents in the Parish Archive provide evidence for this.

6 Archives of Sisters of Mercy Granard and reminiscences of the senior members of the community, especially Sister Mary Patrick Murphy.

7 Registry of Births, Marriages and Deaths, Co. Clinic, Longford.

8 Manuscript records of students, St Mel's College, Longford.

9 *Maynooth College Calendar* and Diocesan Archive.

10 Ibid.

11 Diocesan Archive.

12 Diocesan Archive.

13 Diocesan Archive.

14 Diocesan Archive and Parish Chronicle called 'Chronicon', written by Canon O'Kane and preserved in the Parish Archive of St Mary's, Granard. It will be quoted throughout as 'Chronicon'.

15 Diocesan Archive.

16 Diocesan Archive.

17 Diocesan Archive.

18 Diocesan Archive.

19 'Chronicon', 1952, p. 100, Diocesan Archive.

20 'Chronicon'. Diocesan Archive.

21 Diocesan Archive.

22 'Chronicon', Diocesan Archive.

23 'Chronicon', Diocesan Archive.

24 'Chronicon', Diocesan Archive.

25 Interview with Bishop Colm O'Reilly, 12 January 1994.

26 'Chronicon' *passim*.

27 Interview with Bishop Colm O'Reilly, 12 January 1994.

28 'Chronicon', 1933, p. 15.

29 Archive of Granard Urban District Council, De-urbanisation File, Co. Council Buildings, Longford.

30 De-urbanisation File, Letter to Town Clerk, Granard from Minister for Local Government dated 23 June 1922.

31 Ibid.

32 De-urbanisation File, Letter to Acting Town Clerk, Granard from Secretary, Department of Local Government and Public Health, dated 9 January 1941 enclosing Dissolution Order G26, 344/1940.

33 'Chronicon', 1933, p. 15.

34 De-urbanisation File, Report of Dr McDonnell, 2 November 1928.

35 'Chronicon', 1933, p. 14.

36 'Chronicon', 1935, p. 24.

37 Seamus Helferty and Raymond Refausse (eds), *Directory of Irish Archives* (Dublin, 1993), p. 14.

38 By his Will, dated 24 August 1965, Bishop MacNamee appointed as his executors the Very Revd James Canon Griffin P.P., Newtownforbes, the Very Revd John Lennon, President, St Mel's College, Longford and the Very Revd Alphonsus McGowan, Administrator, St Mel's Cathedral, Longford.

MATERIAL THINGS: PARISH ADMINISTRATION

1 *New Code of Canon Law*, 1983 Canon 515 1.
2 'Chronicon', 1933, p. 11.
3 'Chronicon', 1941, p. 53.
4 'Chronicon', 1955, p. 115.
5 Parish Archive: 'Granard Parish – Census 1953' (Field-Book)
6 Perkin, M. and Blade, R., *Modern macroeconomics* (2nd Edition, Oxford, 1986) p. 162.
7 'Chronicon', 1940, p. 43.
8 A personal Account Book of Canon O'Kane, preserved in the parish archive, has the following illustrative reference to the remuneration given to housekeepers. 'Maureen O'Shea, Fermoyle, Lanesboro, came 19th January, 1953. Wages £5.00 per month with an extra £5.00 at holiday time: 1954 from 03.08 to 22.11. £6.00 per month and after that £7.00 per month. 1955, 56, 57 £7.00 per month: and would not accept more'. She was an experienced housekeeper, having served an apprenticeship at a well-known 'training-school' in Ballinahown, in the south of the diocese. 'Brigid Connell, Ballyboy, Abbeylara, came 26th January, 1953. Wages £3.00 per month.' (There is no reference to any extra at holiday-time). She was an 'improver'. She does not seem to have persevered beyond one year.
9 Interview with a retired priest of the diocese, Very Revd Canon Hubert Fee, who worked under a similar regime in Ferbane.
10 'The main support of the clergy comes, of course, from the rather barbarous system of Funeral Offerings'. 'Chronicon', 1948, p. 85.

SPIRITUAL THINGS: PARISH MINISTRY

1 In 1952 one of the teachers of Killeen school was on the panel for a time, but numbers increased again before she was forced to transfer. Enrolment at Killasonna also gave cause for concern. 'Chronicon', 1952, p. 101.
2 'Chronicon', 1939, p. 39.
3 'Chronicon', 1951, p. 99.
4 'Chronicon', 1951, p. 99.
5 'Chronicon', 1955, p. 116. 'Seven men living in the parish were married: two of them brought wives here and five went to live away from here: twenty-two young people – eleven boys and eleven girls – born in Granard and rather recently emigrated applied for marriage papers to marry in England: three girls (applied for marriage papers) to marry in America and six girls, away from home (applied for marriage papers) to marry in different parts of Ireland. Five men, born here and living in Ireland, got papers for marriage and intend to live in Ireland. A remarkable thing, surely, is that not one girl from the parish and only two men got married to live here.'
6 'Chronicon', 1933, p. 11.
7 'Chronicon', 1938, p. 35.
8 'Chronicon', 1951, p. 99.

PATTERNS OF RELIGIOUS PRACTICE

1 These particulars are printed as Appendix 1 to this Study.
2 'Chronicon', 1939, p. 40.
3 See Table 1 above.
4 'Chronicon', 1933, p. 1.
5 The last Mass in the old Church as offered on Sunday 26th June, 1961 by the parish priest, who regretted that it fell to his lot to see the Church closed in his time ...' 'Chronicon', 1961 p. 133.
6 St Guasacht, The Patron of the Church, was, according to tradition, the son of Milchu, St Patrick's slave-master. St Patrick placed him in charge of the first Christian foundation of Granard. See James J. MacNamee, *History of the diocese of Ardagh* (Dublin, 1954) pp. 34-5 and 646.
7 The Code gives the name of pious

union to a religious congregation or association consisting of lay-persons, male or female, or both male and female, meeting together at stated times under ecclesiastical direction, for the performance of pious exercises, and recommending to each of its members conformity in order to promote the honour of God, devotion to the Blessed Virgin, the spread of good works and the spiritual advancement of those who faithfully observe them. If such a pious union is constituted as an organic body, it is called a sodality. Solality in Thomas Addis, William E. Arnold, T.B. Scannell, P.E. Hallet, *A Catholic dictionary* (London, 1953), pp. 752-3. Also see *Codex Juris Canonici* (1918) Canon 707.

8 'Chronicon', 1933, pp. 4-5.

9 See, for example, Diary of Bishop John Kilduff, Sunday, 27 August 1859, quoted in John Monahan, *Records Relating to the Diocese of Ardagh and Clonmacnois* (Dublin, 1886), p. 255. 'Held Visitation at the chapel of Granardkille. The state of religion is very low in this parish. Many do not frequent the sacraments. Many do not even go to Mass on Sundays …'. 'Chronicon', 1939, p. 39 in reporting Bishop McNamee's address on Confirmation day says he exhorted to better attendance at Sunday mass, Sodalities etc. and warned again about occasions of sin and scandal.

10 In recalling the Parish Mission of 1933, the parish priest wrote: 'Those who needed it most attended worst …' 'Chronicon', 1933, p. 10.

11 In 1933 Ash Wednesday fell on 22 Febraury, Easter Sunday on 9th March and Pentecost on 28 May. Parish Archive: Church Notice Book for years 1935-43.

12 'The members of the women's branch [of the Immaculate Conception Sodality] are not nearly so loyal in attending their general communion (on the Second Sunday of the month) or their meeting on the same evening: but most of them do come to the sacraments

once a month, on the first Friday or on the other Feast days.' 'Chronicon', 1933, p. 4.

13 One fortnight left now for fulfilling Easter Duty: if not yet done, prepare and do not postpone till the last moment. Parish Archive, 'Church notice book 1935-1943' under date 14.5.39.

14 'Sodality' in William E. Addis, Thomas Arnold, T.B. Scannell and P.E. Hallett, *A Catholic Dictionary* (London, 1953) pp. 752-3.

15 The arrangements published in the Church notice-book on Sunday, 11th June 1939 for the *Corpus Christi* Procession to take place that evening at 6p.m. include this statement: 'The Members of the St Vincent de Paul Society and Prefects of the Sodalities will carry the Canopy'. (This would be a special honour). The same announcements gives its own place in the Procession to each of the Sodalities thus singling them out from what it describes as the General Public. Parish Archive: Church Notice-Book 1935-43, under date 11.6.39.

16 'Chronicon', 1933, p. 10.

17 'Chronicon', 1938, p. 35.

18 'Chronicon', 1946, p. 73.

19 Conversations with several elderly people who attended and shared in these Holy Hours.

20 Conversations with various elderly people.

21 Parish Archive: Annual Report 1933, 'Chronicon', p. 11.

22 'Chronicon', 1933, pp. 4-5.

23 'Chronicon', 1933, p. 4.

24 'Chronicon', 1933, p. 5.

25 'Chronicon', 1933, p. 5.

26 'Chronicon', 1933, p. 5. The Murta Charity Fund referred to was a fund established by one James Murta, a native of Granard living in Asutralia, who in 1913 bequeathed to the parish priest for the time being twenty £40 shares in the Bank of Australasia to be sold by him and the proceeds distributed at his descretion amongst such of the poor of the said parish as he shall select.

27 'Chronicon', 1936, p. 27.
28 'Chronicon', 1938, p. 34.
29 'Chronicon', 1949, p. 91.
30 The Canon Dolan Charity was a local charity established from funds left in his will by a native of Granard, Canon Patrick Dolan, who died in January 1933. He had inherited a substantial sum from his brother, a medical director in England, and he bequeathed it for the relief of poverty in his native town.
31 'Chronicon', 1961, p. 140.
32 Interview with Bishop Colm O'Reilly, 12 January 1994.
33 Conversations with senior members of the Association.
34 c.f. 'Chronicon', 1959, p. 132.
35 'Chronicon', 1938, p. 34.
36 'Chronicon', 1955, p. 114.
37 Ibid.
38 'Chronicon', 1936, p. 27.
39 'Chronicon', 1936, p. 27.
40 'Chronicon', 1949, p. 90.
41 See 'Chronicon', 1953, p. 106.
42 'Chronicon', 1957, p. 122.
43 'Chronicon', 1957, p. 122.
44 There are still a good number of people in the parish who attended Patrician meetings as teenagers and some few who attended them as adults. Some from each group have been interviewed.

CONCLUSION

1 'Chronicon', 1940, p. 45.
2 'Chronicon', 1959, p. 132.

APPENDIX I

1 Feast of the Epiphany (6 January): Holyday of Obligation: same mass arrangements as on Sundays.
2 Also, First Friday of the Month, which is a day of special devotion each month in honour of the Most Sacred Heart of Jesus.
3 First Friday of the month: 'Chronicon', 1939, p. 40.
4 Ash Wednesday.
5 First Friday of the month: 'Chronicon', 1939, p. 40.

6 St Patrick's Day: Holyday of Obligation: same mass arrangements as on Sundays.
7 Spy Wednesday.
8 Holy Thursday.
9 Good Friday – no 'First Friday' celebrations this month.
10 Holy Saturday.
11 Easter Sunday.
12 Ascension Day: Holyday of Obligation: same mass arrangements as on Sundays.
13 First Friday of the month: 'Chronicon', 1939, p. 40.
14 Trinity Sunday.
15 Corpus Christi: Holyday of Obligation: same mass arrangements as on Sundays.
16 Feast of the Most Sacred Heart of Jesus.
17 Feast of Saints Peter and Paul: Holyday of obligation (now re-trenched): same mass arrangements as on Sundays.
18 First Friday of the month. 'Chronicon', 1939, p. 40.
19 First Friday of the month; 'Chronicon', 1939, p. 40.
20 Feast of the Assumption of the blessed Virgin Mary. Holyday of Obligation: same mass arrangements as on Sundays.
21 First Friday of the month: 'Chronicon', 1939, p. 40.
22 Feast of the nativity of the Blessed Virgin Mary. Patronal feastday of the parish church.
23 First Friday of the month: 'Chronicon', 1939 p. 40.
24 All Saints Day: Holyday of Obligation: same mass arrangements as on Sundays.
25 All Souls Day.
26 First Friday of the month: 'Chronicon', 1939 p. 40.
27 First Friday of the month: 'Chronicon', 1939 p. 40.
28 Feast of the Immaculate Conception of the Blessed Virgin Mary. Holyday of Obligation: same mass arrangements as on Sunday.
29 Feast of the Nativity of the Lord (Christmas Day): Holyday of Obligation: mass arrangements: midnight, mass 1 and mass 2. The figures for midnight and first masses are given separately, but the figure for Holy Communion is an aggregate.